ADVANCE PRAISE

Crisis hits you when you least expect it. Bill's years of experience and calming disposition truly helped us through a crisis, and his thought process on reputation management is second to none. I would highly recommend Critical Moments to CEOs.

—JOHN KEATING, PRESIDENT OF BUSINESS OPERATIONS
AND SUPPLY CHAIN PROTEIN ENTERPRISE, CARGILL

In a crisis you want a battle-tested veteran. And you want someone like Bill Coletti who can not only put out the immediate fire, but help ensure there is no long-term damage to a firm or individual's reputation. Coletti learned it all the hard way, in the trenches. You can learn it all the easy way by picking up Critical Moments.

—MARK MCKINNON, CREATOR AND COHOST OF
SHOWTIME'S *THE CIRCUS*, AND FORMER MEDIA
ADVISOR TO GEORGE W. BUSH AND JOHN MCCAIN

For any organization today, reputation has never been more critical or less stable. Bill Coletti offers deep experience and plain-spoken wisdom that will help you understand the stakes, navigate the challenges, and make smart decisions while everyone is watching.

I've had the opportunity to work side by side with Bill during high-stakes crises of all stripes. I can say unequivocally, if you're in a fox hole, you will want Bill by your side.

Bill has a deep grasp of the dynamics in our new "reputation economy," and his insight and experience are invaluable to any executive navigating it.

Companies live and die by their reputations. But how to manage reputation? Bill brings much-needed structure to this critical issue.

In the digital world, corporate reputation can change in an instant. Bill Coletti's advice and insights are well worth reading.

—RICHARD CORCORAN, SPEAKER OF THE
FLORIDA HOUSE OF REPRESENTATIVES

Bill was with me as I left one company and started another. His steady hand and careful management with the problems that this caused helped make the transition smooth and the new company successful. I want him at my side whenever things get stormy. As an observer of the global stage and the reputation of the actors therein, I know corporate reputation and elements of trust must be managed for long-term success. Critical Moments is a mustread for CEOs and their teams for its concepts on how reputations are made, lost, and grown.

—GEORGE FRIEDMAN, FOUNDER AND
CHAIRMAN, GEOPOLITICAL FUTURES

Until now, reputation management has been an oxymoron. How do you manage the unmanageable? Bill's 4 As go a long way in creating a framework for success that leaders can follow to make sense of reputation.

—EDWIN MILLER, FOUNDER AND CEO, 9LENSES

Bill does more than a credible job at taking both past and contemporary examples of critical moments and demonstrating how to navigate optimal reputation outcome. There is a genuine tone to the book that makes it easy to read and understand. Love the 4 As.

—BILL HEYMAN, PRESIDENT AND CEO, HEYMAN ASSOCIATES

Bill is what is needed during any critical moment: a calming and smart influence who always thinks two steps ahead.

—KEN LUCE, FOUNDER AND MANAGING
PARTNER, LDWWGROUP

Bill provides valuable advice that every company of every type and size will need at some critical moment in the future.

—MARY SCOTT NABORS, CEO, STRATEGIC
PARTNERSHIPS INC.

Crisis? What crisis? In Critical Moments Bill Coletti shows how proper reputation management allows astute marketers to turn mistakes and other unanticipated events into opportunities.

—BLAIR ENNS, AUTHOR OF *THE WIN WITHOUT
PITCHING MANIFESTO*, AND TWENTY-FIVE-
YEAR VETERAN OF CREATIVE AGENCIES

Bill's approach is methodical, honest, and real. Bill successfully led our family through a crisis that seemed at the time unsurmountable and that garnered national media attention for weeks. His integrity during every step of our journey was not only refreshing but led to a lasting friendship.

—BRODY PETTIT, OWNER AND PRESIDENT,
PETTIT MACHINERY INC.

CRITICAL MOMENTS

CRITICAL MOMENTS

THE NEW MINDSET OF REPUTATION MANAGEMENT

BILL COLETTI

LIONCREST
PUBLISHING

CRITICAL MOMENTS
The New Mindset of Reputation Management

ISBN 978-1-61961-742-1 *Hardcover*
      978-1-61961-676-9 *Paperback*
      978-1-61961-677-6 *Ebook*

To my parents for creating amazing moments throughout my life, and to my girls, I love you. I am proud of the strong confident women you are becoming.

CONTENTS

NOTE TO READERS

For digital resources to unlock your reputation, go to criticalmomentsbook.com.

INTRODUCTION

How many fires have you had to put out today? This week? This year? If you were United Airlines, Uber, or the Trump White House in the summer of 2017, it may have felt like you were doing this every hour. Responding to crises can drain your resources without moving your organization forward. This book seeks to recharge your thinking about what to do before, during, and most importantly, after a crisis, when growing and repairing your reputation is most critical. Managing your reputation may seem like an overwhelming task, but the key message contained in this book is that reputation management can be made manageable. In these pages, you will learn how to stop overfocusing on crises and instead discover practices to help you avoid, manage, and recover from the events that affect your company's reputation.

The way we are used to talking about crisis just doesn't work anymore. In my work as a crisis communication consultant, I often saw businesses trying to catalog risk by organizing every imaginable calamity in a series of white binders. The pages filed inside listed everything from executive plane crashes to data breaches to workplace violence. The examples collected in these binders were never exhaustive and were frequently exhausting to maintain. So, they got compiled, shelved, and forgotten.

I understand the impulse behind these binders. People want to control risk because uncertainty is uncomfortable and overwhelming. I know how they feel. Honestly, as a consultant in years past, I created those binders and plans that ended up sitting on shelves. I realize now that this was the wrong approach; that's not what people need. For those of you I did that to, I'm sorry, and I owe you a signed copy of this book.

When you look at risk this way, you bring to the surface all the things that could go wrong. You're probably overwhelmed by what you see. You also know you don't have the time and energy to respond to every possible scenario. Rarely does the disaster unfold or the public react exactly as you would imagine.

I invite you to move away from the notion of "putting out

fires" and instead view your risks as "critical moments" that offer an opportunity to shape and protect your reputation going forward. With this proactive perspective, you can move out of crisis mode and into creation mode, building an understanding of how your reputation was shaped, how your organization can respond, and how you can seek and attain reputational excellence.

The practice of crisis response is moving away from those once ubiquitous binders and holding statements. This book will not add substantially to the art and tactic of crisis management and response. There are already a number of best practices that companies and practitioners can use to strengthen crisis response. When a natural disaster or tragic industrial accident impacts a community—a true crisis—there are established best practices for responding. It's the same in an organization; when a specific crisis hits, the company likely knows how best to respond. If you did something wrong—apologize and fix it. If the event was external to you - emphasized with the affected community and work to get back to normal—sharing details along the way. A crisis is a singular event created by some sort of stimuli. A crisis is a one-off public disruption to your business as usual. It can be managed with well-established best practices.

Critical moments, by contrast, happen over time and

shape the way the public perceives the organization. Compared to crises, critical moments appear unwieldy. Consider the downward spiral suffered by Uber in 2017 when a series of missteps forced people to question the character of the organization. How do they get that under control? The same sort of thing happened to United Airlines when a customer was dragged off a plane by law enforcement in April 2017. The public is relatively forgiving of crises, but they remember critical moments. That's important because their reaction to critical moments over time is what shapes your organization's reputation.

This book will explore the key distinctions between crises and critical moments and show you how to develop and grow your corporate reputation and improve resilience, leading the way to more successful long-term outcomes.

CRISIS OR CRITICAL MOMENT?

When is a crisis actually a critical moment? What's the difference?

Critical moments affect the deepest levels of your organization's reputation. They're not isolated events, but endemic, DNA-level characteristics of your company. Critical moments inform the public and shape their beliefs about you. Crises are one-off events that can be managed, but critical moments—how you react to them, how you talk about them over the long term—impact your reputation. It's a fine distinction, but it's important because the old vocabulary of crisis doesn't work in reputation management. If we use the old label, "crisis," we're bound to think of bodily injury and natural disaster rather than self-inflicted reputational wounds. We need a new vocabulary to help us focus on the critical moments that shape our image over time.

A recent article (PwC 2017), for instance, highlights the difficulty of relying on an old vocabulary to talk about a new concept. PwC (PricewaterhouseCoopers) surveyed CEOs about how many crises they've faced. Sixty-five percent of respondents said they've faced at least one crisis in the past three years. Over half of them reported going through two or more in the previous year. About 15 percent said they had been hit by five or more crises in the last three years.

These are interesting numbers, but what do they mean? It's impossible to know what definition of crisis the survey respondents had in mind. Were they thinking about financial disasters? Public gaffes? Systemic problems? The PwC study is valuable, but if you dig down, you can see that the responses were wide-ranging. There's no universal definition of crisis. Some of these events might better be described, understood, and leveraged as critical moments.

If you can learn to identify, name, and pay more attention to *critical moments*, you will create opportunities for the growth of your company, your brand, and most importantly, your reputation, far into the future.

Crises are overwhelming. Don't wait until there's a crisis. Use critical moments to shape your future. To get a feeling for how they can be shaped, for better or for worse, let's look at some real-life cases.

CASE STUDY: CHIPOTLE
SUMMER/FALL 2016

The fast-casual restaurant chain Chipotle offers a case in point. When a series of food safety scares left dozens of customers ill and drove the company's share price down dramatically, it was a restaurant's worst nightmare come true. How did Chipotle get into this situation? First, they may have received less scrutiny on food safety issues than others because they were perceived as strong on quality. Second, they were slow to respond when the problem became apparent. And then, they responded dramatically—shutting down forty-three stores within forty-eight hours without ever discussing the root cause of the problem. They managed it as a crisis, as a singular episode involving their sanitation processes, when it really came from a variety of problems in the way they managed their supply chain.

Because they managed the food safety issue as a crisis as opposed to a more comprehensive problem, Chipotle failed to uncover the underlying problem. That failure has allowed the situation to continue beyond the initial outbreak into another one in 2017.

Critical moments are situations that offer a fork in the road. Which path you take may determine whether your business grows significantly or not. Unfortunately, people are, for the most part, better prepared for crises than critical moments.

CASE STUDY: EPIPEN
2004

You probably read the news stories about the dramatic price hikes made by Mylan, the maker of the EpiPen epinephrine auto-injector (Lesak-Greenberg 2016). When Mylan purchased EpiPen nine years ago, the devices cost about $57 each. By May of 2016, EpiPens cost over $600 for a pack of two. Since 2004, adjusting for inflation, the price of EpiPens has risen more than 450 percent. Understandably, customers were angry. Congress called on the CEO to provide testimony, and the company ultimately settled a suit with the Department of Justice and other agencies for $465 million. Mylan's decision clearly backfired, but what was behind it?

Mylan likely had a plan for dealing with a crisis related to its product. They probably knew what to do in the case of a claim of patient harm, for example. They likely went to considerable lengths to make sure users would not be harmed by their product, and to minimize any harm that might happen. They surely had a plan for what to do in a crisis. In hindsight, though, it doesn't seem that Mylan applied the same kind of thoughtful deliberation when it raised the price. On paper, it looks like a great way to increase profit, but Mylan apparently failed to adequately consider how this decision would align—or misalign—with the values of their communities, customers, and critics. Mylan did not appear to think as carefully about this critical moment in the company's development as they must have thought about crisis management.

How could they have done better? That's a key question we will address throughout this book, as we explore concepts and techniques that can broaden our focus from the limited concept of managing crises to a broader perspective that acknowledges the power of critical moments

to transform and maintain a company's reputation over
the long term.

CASE STUDY: SBC
JANUARY 2005

Coming to a fork in the road can be daunting. Some
companies manage it well, though. In January 2005, my
team and I worked with regional telecommunications
provider SBC as they planned to merge with and acquire
their former parent company, AT&T. By buying AT&T,
an iconic American brand, SBC Communications would
significantly expand its reach, becoming the biggest long-
distance carrier in America. But how was SBC going to
grow and transform the telecom marketplace? This was
their critical moment.

SBC faced huge risks, including increased competition
from other "Baby Bell" companies, but they recognized
that this moment also came with an incredible opportunity. The deal promised the newly formed company
annual sales of $70 billion. Closing the deal could paralyze
their business, or it could spur tremendous growth. The
lead negotiator for SBC had a clear vision of the synergy
among the companies, as well as SBC's financial capabil-
ities. He was thinking not just about numbers, but also
how they could convince the public, through regulators

and elected officials, that the deal was truly in customers' and consumers' best interest. He understood the
critical moment.

Had they instead moved in recklessly, SBC could have
suffered financial and reputation losses and could have
risked public safety. The people closest to a decision must
consider both internal business rationale and outside
reaction. The deal went through in January of 2005. After
the merger, SBC retained the well-known and valuable
AT&T brand.

CASE STUDY: FREQUENT-FLYER ALLIANCES
APRIL 2011

I led a team who worked with American Airlines at a critical moment. American ran a frequent-flyer program called
One World that was competing against Delta's SkyTeam
for an alliance with Japan Airlines. Japan Airlines had
just reverted to state ownership, and the government
was evaluating the alliance partners they would choose
globally. Of course, we wanted them to choose our client.

We put together a campaign, using campaign-like activities to highlight the features and benefits of the alliance
partnership alongside skillful negotiations and financial
concession. It was vitally important—clearly a critical

moment—to win this deal, remain Japan Airlines's alliance partner, and fend off Delta.

Losing the deal would have had a significant effect on American's Asian business and how it moves passengers globally. If they had lost, it would have crippled their business in Asia. Instead, American Airlines ultimately won.

CASE STUDY: SAN ANTONIO SPURS
SPRING 2008

Some critical moments can be managed by one party, but often, there are several players at the table. When the AT&T Center in San Antonio, home of the NBA team, the Spurs, needed an upgrade, the process mattered to a lot of people. The refurbishment was important to the community, the basketball team, the city, and especially the adjacent rodeo facility.

I led a campaign to help get funding from taxpayer dollars through a bed and occupancy tax on tourists and one on rental cars. The campaign required arriving well-prepared at a series of inflection points—critical moments—with the city. We worked through a ballot initiative. At each turning point, we needed to make it clear how important the team, facility, and the ballot's other proposed improvements were to the community.

Critical moments are always part of the bigger picture; managing them takes sustained effort and a broad perspective.

CASE STUDY: TREK BICYCLE
APRIL 2008

Sometimes, seizing a critical moment means averting crisis. Take Trek Bicycle's well-publicized break with bicyclist Greg LeMond in the spring of 2008, for example (Frothingham 2008). LeMond bikes were a small but significant part of Trek's portfolio. Additionally, Trek had a close and extremely beneficial relationship with Lance Armstrong, whom LeMond publicly criticized.

Trek realized it had to break away from LeMond to preserve the Armstrong relationship—this was before Armstrong's own public reputational meltdown—and they did so in an intentional way. They created a narrative that explained the separation from LeMond and delivered it on their own terms.

The critical moment was the separation. It did not become a crisis because it was planned, reasoned, and rolled out deliberately. It might have been a crisis for the LeMond bike company, but for Trek, it was a critical moment they needed to get right.

These are but a few examples of how critical moments can make or break companies. These moments shape the future. While some are born out of crisis, all have the unique feature of imprinting reputational markers on the stakeholders they care about. Getting ready, managing, and focusing beyond the response is the theme of this book—creating a new mindset of reputation management.

A NEW FRAMEWORK
ABOUT RISK MANAGEMENT

Developing a comprehensive crisis plan can feel like trying to boil the ocean. You may stay awake at night considering worst-case scenarios and trying to prepare for every possible outcome. It's overwhelming, if not impossible.

Communicating possible threats to your organization or team can seem just as impossible. You don't want to come across like Chicken Little crying out that the sky is falling. Plus, you're probably busy trying to instill a can-do, optimistic culture in your people, so focusing on the negative feels counterintuitive.

To prepare your organization for real and potential threats, you need a framework and a language that leaders can understand and effectively communicate throughout the organization.

Most corporations consist of operations (the makers) and communications (the sellers). Each has a different view of risk; there are some things the "operators" understand, manage, and evaluate that the "communicators" know nothing about and vice versa.

Imagine a communications leader going to talk to operations. They bring a blank piece of paper and say, "Tell me everything you think that can go wrong." Alternatively, the approach could be, "I want to talk about strategic risks, things we are doing that may have implications for the public. Let's talk about things you never want to have happen and things you're worried about externally." The conversation will be very different and have vastly different outcomes.

Many communications leaders come from a background in journalism, liberal arts, or English, while most operational people hail from a business background, so it's not surprising that their communications can be at odds. This is certainly not universal—there are a number of people quite talented in both areas—but these backgrounds frequently color conversations between colleagues, which may leave both parties bewildered and the mission—real risk management—incomplete. Maybe they finish with a list they can take to the general counsel, who will ask them to make additions. Then, they have a longer list, but no one has really aligned around common issues. A better conversation would provide both sides with greater knowledge and empowerment.

REFRAMING RISK

I've spent much of my career running from fire to fire. Some were large and others small. Some fires involved loss of life; others had massive, game-changing financial implications. Many were choices that could spur growth or paralyze a business. I knew there had to be a simpler framework that could set the tone for an appropriate response that minimized damage and maximized outcome.

I spent the early part of my career doing political campaigns and working with elected officials. From 1986 to 2001, I was involved in various political campaigns and worked directly with politicians and elected officials from across the country and internationally. There were all sorts of crises and critical moments in those situations. Most political campaigns hop from critical moment to critical moment to critical moment because both sides are trying to push the other side's buttons. I was constantly reacting to elected officials, their successes and failures, and the implications of their policies and the public's perceptions.

In 2000 I started working with a high-level strategic-communications firm that applied political-campaign skills to corporations. We encouraged the same kind of strategic thinking in the public arena that was common among lawyers, investment bankers, accountants, and management consultants. There was room at the table for a fifth participant: someone thinking about public implications and involved in strategic risk-planning. Our firm helped them bake the concept of the public into their thought processes.

We evolved through a reverse merger into a larger, global public relations firm, where I noticed that corporations, much like politicians, tended to bounce from problem to problem and crisis to crisis. I came in again as a firefighter, running from fire to fire. Some companies were prepared, but others were not, and that had game-changing implications for the company's future. Working this way, people lost their jobs and businesses failed. I knew there should be a better way to prepare and to plan. These crises, had we thought about them in advance, could have instead been opportunities to expand and grow.

As I moved to my own firm, Kith, in 2013, I continued thinking in this vein and started looking at risk. In 2012 I read a *Harvard Business Review* article about looking at risk from a financial standpoint and had an aha moment (Kaplan and Mikes 2012). The article was called, "Managing Risk: A New Framework," and after reading it, as well as doing additional research, I became much more empowered around the concepts of risk. I asked myself who had risk figured out, and the answer was the financial industry. (Regarding the 2000 financial crisis, the movie *The Big Short* and the related book *Liar's Poker* make it clear that risk was known in the run up to the crisis. The warnings were ignored. That is the fault of the market participants, not the framework to evaluate risk.) Risk managers and committees evaluate financial risk in structural terms. Here was the beginning of a new vocabulary around risk. The focal point needed to be on the strategy and controllability of the risk and, therefore, the public perception.

If you think of risks as belonging to one of three categories—strategic (seeking to grow enterprise value), preventable (offering no strategic benefit), or external (outside of your control)—you can familiarize everybody in the company with the risks in a way that fits their role. Shaping messaging around these categories simplifies and streamlines the communications-planning process.

STRATEGIC RISK

A strategic risk is an intentional risk a company chooses to take for a significant investment return. Imagine that a company that makes and packages hamburger patties decides to reduce the frequency of preventive maintenance on their conveyer belts. Because the machine has always worked perfectly, they predict that the reduced maintenance will save resources. This decision must be weighed against the possibility that something could go wrong, causing physical contaminants to fall into the product. When the company decides to go ahead with the reduced maintenance plan because of overall cost savings and workflow improvement, they're taking a strategic risk.

PREVENTABLE RISK

While taking strategic risks requires a balancing act, I recommend a zero-tolerance policy for preventable risks. These threats come from within the company and generate no economic benefit. Blue Bell Creameries offers a cautionary tale here. In 2015 Blue Bell experienced the pains of not having rigorous enough standards in place when an outbreak of Listeria resulted in three deaths and many illnesses. Blue Bell had to pull its products from stores and put more robust testing procedures in place. Customers expect you to keep your promises, and they remember when you fail to come through. Blue Bell's reputation suffered in this situation.

EXTERNAL RISK

Sometimes, even with the best internal preparation, an unexpected event can wreak havoc on your plans. External risks are, by definition, out of your control. These are things that happen to you—a hurricane destroys your facilities, a never-heard-of pathogen enters the food supply chain, or an active shooter holds hostages in one of your restaurants. This last event really happened to Luby's Restaurants, a Texas chain. Companies can't do much to prevent these types of scenarios from taking place, but they can be prepared to respond effectively to protect the brand and public perception.

EVOLUTION OF THE FOUR A'S

While this new framework was on my mind, I was working with the College Board on a specific issue that further illuminated the need for a new approach to reputation management. Planning challenges in rolling out a new score delivery system was limiting the way educators in schools were accessing the data. While on a particularly long flight back from a visit with the College Board, I looked at the two events and thought: the inefficient delivery of test results is a preventable risk. It's not an external risk, like a hurricane arriving on test day or a delivery truck getting robbed. There should be zero tolerance for not taking a user-centric approach; with proper, prudent planning, the problem could be entirely avoided. I realized we had to figure out how to think about these types of risk in a logical way that would let us be better prepared.

The framework I now work with, after twenty-five years in corporate and political communications, evolved from these beginnings. I found that people came to us in one of four situations. Some came in the middle of a crisis, saying, "My house is on fire, and I need help now." Others had already put out the proverbial fire and wanted help rebuilding. Still others had noticed that their neighbor's house was on fire and wanted to find out how to make sure they weren't next in line. Finally, a segment of clients came to us knowing that fire was possible, but they were essentially prepared for it. These folks were looking beyond the crisis; they wanted to expand and grow their reputations. This last domain is what this book is about.

Navigating Through Critical Moments

Our firm often gets called in to help companies in a critical moment. We would manage that moment with tools and tactics that would help the client come out breathing a sigh of relief: we survived. We fixed the problem, stopped the bleeding. Next came a debriefing conversation: What do we do now? How do we improve our reputation? I advocated for taking the next step toward reputation building so they would be more resilient and ready when something similar happened again. Everybody said, "Yeah, I want some of that reputation stuff. That's important."

Clients usually did not have a solid framework for understanding reputation, though. They often felt reputation management was essentially a marketing function. In those days, without a model to work with, I would try to fend off that notion, telling them that brand and reputation are two very different things. But, they would respond, "Isn't reputation management just good PR or good press?" I would explain that it is about building trust in people, even people who don't necessarily have a stake in your company or your product, but who will impact your reputation nonetheless.

A classic example is BP's oil-platform accident in the Gulf of Mexico. One of the easiest ways to explain what we do in crisis and reputation management is to mention BP. Whether people used BP products or not, they had opinions about that incident in the Gulf. BP was once an incredibly successful company. I remember working for Amoco in 1998 when BP bought them in a $48.2 billion deal. They were huge. Now, five years after the darkest moment in its one-hundred-year history, BP is still a lightning rod for those who are opposed to the oil and gas industry on environmental, social, and moral grounds.

Even with explanations like this, leaders did not necessarily integrate the concept of reputation management into their processes. They needed something concrete to work with. One CEO asked me for a framework or model that would help him move from traditional marketing ideas—like the Four P's: Price, Product, Place, and Promotion—into reputation management. To shift thinking to what I was quickly realizing was the truth—a company owns its brand, but the public owns its reputation—I realized we needed a unique framework for understanding. Leaders needed a model that helped them understand the elements of reputation the same way they understood the parts of the marketing mix.

That realization led me to develop the Four A's as a means to make reputation management manageable. Previously, leaders had a variety of tools and tactics available but nothing that fit into a larger, smarter model. Now, with the Four A's of reputation management, they have a blueprint for turning critical moments into reputation-building opportunities for durable, long-term growth.

This perfect storm revealed a larger vision to me. I realized you could put all of these critical moments together in a framework. Even that's just the beginning; it's not the endgame. The endgame is: How do we manage these moments? How do we create and understand risk in a framework, and then, how do we transition to growing reputation as a strategic asset? That epiphany gave rise to the Four A's for reputation management, which are the focus of Part 2 of this book: Awareness, Assessment, Authority, and Action. This is the first time there's been a paradigm for practitioners. Reputation no longer has to be seen as unmanageable.

IN THIS BOOK

What will you find in this book? You'll find a journey, a progression through the foundational concepts in reputation management to an understanding of appropriate actions to take for a successful future.

In Part 1, you'll learn what reputation management is and is not and why it's so important to your business. This foundation is crucial and not only theoretical. You'll also discover specific ways you can affect your reputation and how to work with the players involved in a sustained reputation management effort. Finally, you'll consider the context of reputation management today in light of traditional branding and marketing concepts.

We need to refine the way we look at crises and critical moments and understand the impact that has on reputation. In Part 1 of this book, we'll introduce a new perspective and examine a new paradigm you can use to set up a reputation management system in your organization in order to bring the necessary structure to bear on the journey to a robust and resilient reputation.

In Part 2, we'll drill down into the components of the new paradigm, the Four A's: Awareness, Assessment, Authority, and Action. You will see how each element builds on the others and you'll learn why it's so important to do the foundational work of reputation management before choosing Action steps. Let's make your first steps just that—first steps on a sustained journey to reputational excellence for you and your business.

PART 1

UNLOCKING THE POTENTIAL OF REPUTATION MANAGEMENT

CHAPTER ONE

———

WHAT IS REPUTATION?

"Reputation is what people expect us to do next. It's their expectation of the quality and character of the next thing we produce or say or do."

SETH GODIN, AUTHOR, ENTREPRENEUR AND MARKETER

What is reputation, anyway?

I like the definition Michael Barnett wrote when he was at the Centre for Corporate Reputation at Oxford University's Saïd Business School. He said "corporate reputation" is an:

> ...observers' collective judgments of a corporation based on assessments of the financial, social, and

environmental impacts attributed to the corporation over time.

Here's what speaks to me: reputation is about observers and the particular elements they observe. Also, reputation depends on how the observers' judgments of those elements accumulate over time.

Seth Godin offers a similar perspective on reputation with an emphasis on moving into the future. Godin says reputation is "what people expect us to do next. It's their expectation of the quality and character of the next thing we produce or say or do." He defines the things people evaluate—quality and character—and frames them in terms of expectations.

NEXPECTATIONS

My definition of reputation draws and expands on those ideas. I say that the company owns its brand, but the public owns its reputation. Reputation is ultimately based on the expectation of what a company will do next, which is based on the public's perception of what the company has done repeatedly over time, and that's why it is so hard to change. One action, one comment, or one press statement will not improve it. A company's reputation flows both ways in time: past actions create an impression and set the stage for what people expect it to do next. These "nexpectations" define a company's reputation.

Consider a company like Walmart. People have built a set of expectations around Walmart over time. They're not all true—they've become corporate legend. Customers expect Walmart to offer lots of product choice at incredibly low prices. Employees expect less-than-ideal pay. Suppliers expect Walmart to be difficult to accommodate. Whether these statements are true or not, customers, suppliers, and the public assume these elements are intrinsic to Walmart, so they expect more of the same in the future. The irony is that Walmart does a lot of terrific things, like developing solar facilities to power stores with renewable energy. Their commitment to solar power began with their first on-site United States solar installation in 2007. They quickly became the top commercial solar energy user and have been recognized by the EPA's Green Power Partnership. Presidents Bill Clinton and Barack Obama each visited a Mountain View, California, Walmart to acknowledge the role of renewable energy in America's future. They also are making real strides in increasing pay for associates as part of a two-year, $2.7 billion investment in workers (Walmart 2016).

BRAND VS. REPUTATION

The work we do with companies helps them communicate their reputation to the various publics important to them. It's a different process from marketing. Marketing primarily involves putting your product or service in front of the right customers and drawing them closer. Marketing focuses on sales, revenue, and growth. Brand, too, describes products and services, as well as people's experience interacting with the company. Companies can control those interactions. They might manage the way a product looks in packaging, how easily it's procured, or the way a retail or online interaction unfolds.

Reputation, on the other hand, refers to the perceptions of people who have not interacted with the products or services per se but have still made a judgment based on their ideas about the company. A company can reinforce and grow its reputation but is very much dependent upon this intangible relationship, as opposed to the tangible relationship people have with the products or services it sells. The distinction is whose behavior we are trying to impact. If we're trying to impact a customer, we have total control. If we're trying to impact the public, we have less control. That's what makes reputation management so much more difficult.

Think about a company that has enjoyed a tremendously positive reputation: Apple. Apple is known and loved for its reputation as an innovative, forward-thinking company.

Apple continues to grow and innovate, but some recent perception studies show that Apple is losing a bit of its coolness. According to an annual study by the Reputation Institute, Apple is experiencing a slow but certain deterioration in perceived corporate reputation with significant decline over the past year (Campbell 2017). The reason for Apple's decline was not immediately clear, but the Reputation Institute's CMO Allen Bonde says the company's ranking has been falling since it finished in the number two spot in 2011, reports CNET (Musil 2017). "Apple still has an excellent reputation for its products and corporate performance, but as the perceptions of its governance and citizenship fade, the company is starting to take a hit when it comes to its overall corporate reputation," Bonde said. Apple believers continue to love their products, but they're starting to have opinions about Apple that are not as adoring as they once were. Apple, of course, has been so dramatically transformational and innovative for so long that it has a steep hill to keep climbing.

You know how friends and family come to expect certain behaviors? If you've always been the first person to order dessert and now you're embarking on a weight-loss program, people might be shocked when you skip the chocolate mousse. It's not what they expect. People persist in listening to their old tapes. You might make a positive change, and nobody will acknowledge it. Say you used to be difficult to work with, but you've developed some new skills that make interacting with you much easier. People still expect the old behavior, and it might take them a long time to fully recognize the change. Personal reputation can often be hard to budge.

The same is true for corporate reputations. It's difficult and can take a long time to change perceptions. It can be done, though. Walmart is an example of a company that's working diligently to change perceptions, but it takes a number of impressions, made over and over again, before the new reputation takes hold. Walmart could change people's perceptions of a specific product or brand with a slick ad, but that won't fundamentally change the public's overall opinion of the company. Making that kind of sea change takes a long, sustained initiative. After all, it took a long time to develop the first set of expectations. It makes sense that it will take time to change them.

You can't just talk the talk; you really have to walk the walk. If you look at the reputation management pyramid, you'll see a thick blue line right under the word "Action." This represents the final transition after you've built a foundation for that action. You can't just go "do" reputation. Sure, you can hold a press conference, issue a press release, pitch reporters, and reach out to influencers, but these are incremental steps in climbing the reputation mountain. The process builds through the Four A's, from Assessment to Awareness to Authority to Action. Staying the course requires sustained commitment to authentic goals. You can't jump the blue line; you must prepare. Otherwise, you'll waste undifferentiated resources and time seeking change before you build a strong foundation on which to grow.

The 4 A's of Reputation Excellence

What's the difference between good PR and reputation management? This is a common question and an area where much misunderstanding occurs. Reputation management and good PR can be thought of like health care. It's the difference between a broken arm that requires a cast and heart disease, which demands long-term dietary and lifestyle changes. Think about conventional public relations work. It's very transactional and organized around a specific audience, perhaps certain stakeholders. PR is also episodic, revolving around moments in time. Reputation management, on the other hand, must be sustained over time and across multiple audiences you don't have direct control over. That sustainability is directly related to who controls reputation, and that's the public.

Let's look at Google as an example. Google, or more properly, Alphabet, has the number-one browser and email service. Chrome and Gmail are easy to use; millions of people use both services to store their information. User confidence is high. Still, Google is not immortal. If they were to have a data breach like the one that affected Yahoo in 2016, their ecosystem of goodwill would be significantly drawn down. If Google introduced new products following an adverse reputation event like a breach, it would face skepticism and friction because of damage done to their reputation. Even a successful company like this needs to make sure that its systems truly protect its reputation and can't be ruined by one negative user experience.

Companies that sell the Trump brand faced tough decisions about their reputations in light of the 2016 presidential election. Many sellers of Trump merchandise faced boycotts. Customers boycotting the brand also called sellers out in public. Many set up websites. One, called grabyourwallet.org, kept a log of the different companies selling Trump products. A number of companies have decided it's in their best interest to stop participating in that space. Companies like Nordstrom have decided to move away from the Trump name. That's a reputation decision because it takes into consideration people's perceptions of what the president does and the impact those products have on particular companies.

You can't fix reputation with a price reduction or improved packaging, just like you can't fix your personal reputation issues by changing your hair color. Your reputation is about who you are. Reputation requires constant attention, but there's a process to manage it, which we'll look closely at when we detail the Four A's. Essentially, it's a deliberate, intentional process that goes to the heart of the company. It's not reactive.

You can't make someone your friend by offering certain

perks. Instead, if you and the other person both present your authentic selves, a relationship will develop over time. People use the term "fast friends" to talk about instant bonding experiences, but I think those are rare. It generally takes time to develop a relationship.

Similarly, truly great companies are not built to be the flavor of the week. Certainly, some businesses go for rapid return and instant gratification. The best, though, are willing and able to articulate what they stand for and why. People become attracted to that over time.

THE POWER OF PRESENCE

Harvard professor Amy Cuddy talks about what attracts people in terms of personal relationships in her book *Presence* (Cuddy 2015). Her research shows that your presence stems from truly believing in who you are and trusting your feelings, values, and abilities. Presence depends on you being an authentic person, because if you don't trust yourself, you can't really trust others.

Cuddy's discoveries about personal relationships offer insights into corporate reputation. It doesn't matter if you are talking about a conversation between two people or a speech given to a room of five thousand people: authenticity is key. This is equally true if you're interviewing for a job or negotiating a raise. In all of these situations, presence gives you the ability to rise up in the moment. Just like people, companies need to be authentic if they are to respond skillfully to their critical moments.

A reputation is made up of a series of critical moments that shape and mold it over an extended period. It's much like working with a piece of clay, molding it into what's meant to be in the end. Whether you use your thumb or a tool, you shape the clay with a series of very small, individual movements. You may not notice all the individual strokes, but you still shape the clay. Even while you're making tiny adjustments, you keep the whole piece in mind. It won't pay to overemphasize one kind of motion, and you need to pay attention over time to make modifications to your process if needed. No individual movement makes the piece, but when they all get added together, they make a complete work of art. Even then, the artist will evaluate their work and plan to incorporate appropriate changes into the next piece.

It's a never-ending process, much like reputation management. It's also an incredibly important process for business, because, while many companies will continue to sell products and do good things, the select few that really make a mark are those that continually strive for reputational excellence. Reaching these heights gives companies the license to expand into new businesses and also the benefit of the doubt in critical moments. If problems arise, people will say, "Well, that's not the company I know." They'll have faith in the company, which affords the space to make a course-correction. A strong reputation increases a company's resilience.

People make mistakes. Companies make mistakes. But your reputation can help you retain your license to operate and move into new areas. If and when something bad happens, you can respond quickly and draw on the reservoir of goodwill you've built up.

WHAT CAN COMPANIES DO?

Companies have control over the brand experience. You can manage the different touchpoints that shape customers' impressions: lighting, fragrance, sights, and sounds in a retail store, for example. Online, companies like Amazon and Uber work to make transactions seamless. B2B companies can streamline reorders and improve supply chain efficiency. You can do all of these things— and you should—but they don't get to the heart of your reputational challenges.

Distracted by what they can control directly, leaders often lose focus on larger, intangible assets. That's when companies fail to thrive. You may think you have everything in place, but your company doesn't grow and expand. Your systems and processes may be effective, but you stumble when missteps are made. Uber is a timely example: as of this writing, they've made a series of missteps that are not about their technology or process but about the policies, practices, and procedures that affect the company over the long term. By putting effective policies, practices, and procedures in place, you can engrain reputation-thinking into decision-making and everything you do as a company.

Companies make decisions every day that make apparent business sense but have negative effects on their reputations. Look at Microsoft's decision to embed Internet Explorer in every Windows operating system it sold. It seemed to be a solid business decision, a perfect brand decision, but users balked, and regulators reacted in Europe and the United States. The perception was that Microsoft was forcing the product onto consumers who did not necessarily want it. In 2014 Microsoft asked its users to switch to Internet Explorer 11 because they would no longer be providing security patches for the old browser. This may have had a negative impact on the browser usage and may have forced many consumers to begin using Google's Chrome browser, which is much more stable and offers a variety of features to users. Now, we've seen Google's Chrome browser capture 80 percent of the market, while Internet Explorer flounders in the low double digits.

If a company can control its product and manage its brand, that's great. Reputation doesn't work the same way. Reputation is shaped not just by customers but by the public. So, while companies have become incredibly efficient at marketing—it's a data-driven, analytical science—they also need to develop a different skill set. Building reputation requires listening, empathy, and care. It requires being authentic about who you are as a company over the long term.

Some people think the same discipline that's been applied to marketing needs to be applied to reputation, but that's problematic because reputation is an intangible asset. Companies need a new framework for managing a very different beast. There is something you can do about it; all is not lost. The place to start is to understand what you can understand. In the next chapter, we'll explore the dimensions, or levers, that companies can pull to impact their reputations.

CHAPTER TWO

———————

DOING GOOD
AND GETTING
CREDIT FOR IT

*"Public relations means doing good
and getting credit for it."*

DAVID HYATT, VETERAN PUBLICIST

In his book, *Introduction to Public Relations: A Practical Guide as Applied to Industrial and Labor Relations* (1950), veteran publicist David Hyatt defines public relations as "doing good and getting credit for it." Many people feel they are doing good but *not* getting credit for it. Getting that credit—for things they may already be doing—will help them grow their reputation.

Since working in crisis, I've met with a number of CEOs and company leaders who want to grow their company's reputation, but they don't know how. They may already be doing things they're proud of, but few people recognize their efforts. Getting credit without crowing is a delicate tightrope to walk. In order to seek credit without crowing, you need to address the issues and concerns of your key stakeholders in a real way so that the solutions you seek and the solutions you promote are meaningful to not just you but to those you serve. An example of this is what Cargill Protein has started doing with their Cargill Leadership Series.

After doing some initial research with stakeholders, Cargill defined a basket of issues that were of concern to their employees, customers, and the corporation. With that basket in hand, they addressed each issue with key insights and industry observations on the topic, examples of what was being done to work on it collaboratively, and recommendations on best practices. This had the dual benefit of addressing customers' challenges and problems. Additionally, it allowed Cargill to get credit for some of the true leadership and good work they were doing, but it was a delicate balance. Credit was not leading the conversation—solving a problem or addressing a concern was driving the conversation.

Even when companies do the right things, they may not be equally recognized for their actions. Consider Unilever, the packaged goods company, and BMW, the automotive company. Both are industry leaders in the area of social responsibility. Their peers and stakeholders see them as leaders in sustainability.

BMW, though, earned greater recognition for their work than Unilever, even though research shows that Unilever did more work that had a greater impact (Visser 2012). The difference was that BMW talked about it a little bit more than Unilever. While Unilever did good work and was regarded as truly a leader in this space, they didn't promote it as much.

That was a strategic decision for each company, and I can't comment on whether that was right or wrong in either case, but the example shows that there is a way to get credit for doing the work that you're doing. It starts with doing the work first. You have to do the work. Cargill's approach was straightforward—they met the needs, achieved the objectives, and got the credit. BMW and Unilever both did the work, but ironically the one that did more got less credit.

Companies today often launch public relations campaigns to get credit for things they're already doing, whether it's manufacturing an innovative product or posing a sophisticated solution to a global challenge. Companies rightly seek acknowledgment from their key stakeholders; they know that credit can turn into profit.

Timing is also important. In a critical moment, companies may instinctually overreact and rush to highlight the good things they're doing out of a sense of urgency. In desperation, they seek a narrative to fill the vacuum that's been created by the critical moment. Those attempts very often miss the mark because the marketplace is not ready to give credit during or right after the critical moment.

Without deep understanding and awareness of your current position and a strong assessment of the situation, you can't simply toot your own horn. This one-off shot-in-the-dark reaction often misses the mark and winds up doing more harm than good.

The process of reputation management is a journey. We'll talk a lot in this book about the journey to Action that requires you to build a foundation before you act. You can't just jump to the top of the pyramid. Certainly, a critical moment is not the time to do it. You must first develop an Awareness and Assessment of your marketplace, your own needs, your competitors' skill, and your customers' needs.

THE SEVEN LEVERS OF REPUTATION MANAGEMENT

So, how do you get the credit you deserve? Although I've

talked at length about the complexities of reputation management as a concept, I haven't yet introduced concrete steps you can take. There are predictable, practical things you can do to make a difference. In fact, there are seven specific levers that companies can pull to impact reputation.

The seven levers idea grew from studies at Harris Interactive and the Research Institute and work I did at my old firm. Just as you can pull certain levers in marketing (like adjusting the price or dramatically increasing advertising spending) to get people's attention for your products, you can use these seven levers to bring about change in your company's reputation over time. These are the true drivers of reputation.

Levers to Pull for Reputation (Growth)

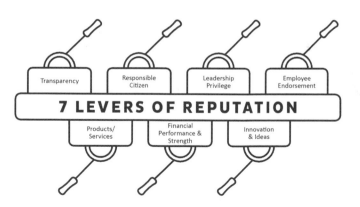

WHY SEVEN?

The work around the dimensions of reputation is a debated subject in the reputation work done to date. Some think there are as few as six dimensions, and others say there are as many as fifteen. I don't intend to jump into the middle of that. The point is that reputation is not one perception but is made up of various touchpoints. Reputation management can be broken down into its subcomponents, making it easier for managers to implement a plan. Based on my experience and the companies I have worked with, these seven represent the best baseline in real-world settings for the dimensions or levers companies can pull. These levers represent the most tangible and useful methods for corporate managers seeking to grow and earn credit using reputation.

The number seven isn't written in stone. When we worked with a major international not-for-profit to evaluate their reputation, we began the process by dimensionalizing it with the seven levers. They determined that one of those dimensions was just not appropriate for the nature of their organization, and that was fine. They chose to focus on six because of the business that they're in. That's an example of why the debate around how many dimensions there are is one for academia. It's not necessarily practically applied. You have to break down reputation into smaller subparts if you're ever going to begin to manage it.

1. QUALITY AND RELIABILITY

Make products and sell services that the public values. Stand behind those products and services. Reputation is not specifically about product features and benefits—that is a function of operations, marketing, and other aspects of the corporation—but a general sense of product or service quality and reliability plays a part in reputation. Without basic quality, your reputation has nothing to grow on. For customers, the first tangible interaction they have with your company is the product or service you sell. That product or service needs to meet a minimum (ideally much greater) level of quality and effectiveness.

Note that negative experiences with content related to your products can significantly impact reputation. Eighty-seven percent of consumers say they would be unlikely or very unlikely to make a repeat purchase with a retailer that provided inaccurate product information (Shotfarm 2016).

AUTOMOBILE RELIABILITY

There has been a general perception shaped over time that Japanese cars are more reliable than American cars and certainly more so than Korean brands such as Hyundai and Kia. Current data does not support this outdated claim, but the perception persists. These attitudes are a critical part of what holds back some of these brands, while perceptions of BMW and Mercedes are very high.

What makes the difference in perception? According to studies by Hirotaka Takeuchi and John Quelch (1983), criteria include straightforward measurements of quality—reliability and performance—but also things like the company's brand name, the store's reputation, and the results of published test results. Perception of quality must be reinforced before, during, and after the sale.

2. INNOVATION AND IDEAS

Encourage ideas and solutions to solve your customer's problems. Be a problem-solving leader for your industry partners. How can you encourage innovation and ideas? Are you constantly creating new products and innovating your systems? Innovation can be displayed through technology, but this kind of forward-looking mindset must be baked into how your company thinks about things. Are you willing to consider rolling out progressive family leave policies for your workers, for instance? Your public is paying attention to the way your company reacts to questions like this. How do you solve problems—not just for yourself but for others?

AMAZON CATALYST

The Amazon Catalyst project is an innovative idea of Amazon's to fund up to $50,000 in moonshot research projects. These are research projects that have been under-appreciated—maybe they're in the early stages—and they haven't been able to achieve funding. Amazon, through the Catalyst program, seeks to be on the vanguard of innovation. They've already had some interesting successes, including a product called Space Shot. Space Shot is a cap that attaches to multidose medication vials and sanitizes needles, preventing the spread of blood disease. It's reusable and significantly reduces the cost of healthcare.

HOBBY LOBBY

The second example is a little bit more controversial, but it relates to Hobby Lobby and their litigation against the Obama Administration and healthcare reform about the government mandate for employer-provided contraceptives. Regardless of where you are on the morality or legality of that issue, Hobby Lobby is leading with an idea and funding that idea in order to seek resolution all the way to the Supreme Court. That significantly impacts their reputation. It has nothing to do with the crafting retail industry. It's about standing up for something they firmly believe in that's authentic to them.

3. WORKFORCE ENDORSEMENT

Make sure the people who work for you are willing to endorse you. Many employee satisfaction studies ask questions like, "Would you refer someone to work here?"

This gets to the heart of the issue of employee endorsement. Without a level of understanding about how your employees view your company, it would be foolish to execute a series of internal communications that only gives lip service to the concept. Do your employees solidly recognize and support your mission and take pride in what their company is doing for society? Your workforce is your team. If you provide an appealing place to work, the individuals who make up your labor force will be willing to give you credit. Treat people well, and they will speak favorably of you. They do not necessarily have to be happy, but they should respect and view you as a good, honest, smart business.

GLASSDOOR.COM

A quick look at Glassdoor.com, the website where employees and former employees can leave anonymous comments about companies, will tell you that strong reputations are closely correlated to employees' willingness to endorse the company. Additionally, favorable ratings for CEOs directly impact how companies are regarded. The CEO of Clorox, Benno Dorer, and his 99 percent approval ranking illustrate how employee endorsement is a building block of reputation.

4. TRANSPARENCY

Obey the law and act ethically. Be transparent about your business practices, and state as much as you can publicly. How responsibly is the company run? Is it a good business partner? Are you open, honest, and fair? How do you make your products? People expect and appreciate openness about these questions. Can you offer too much information? Don't worry about it. People don't need to see it all; if they know it's there, you will get the benefit.

PATAGONIA

Patagonia exemplifies transparency with *The Footprint Chronicles*, a series of videos illustrating the implications of their supply chain on the globe. Customers can access the videos through Patagonia's website and see the environmental impact of their supply chain, good and bad. Users can click on website links to see where different products are sourced, where textile mills and sewing facilities are located. People can see how, where, and when things are made. The company is using video to tell this story in a very transparent way.

5. RESPONSIBLE CITIZENSHIP

Positively impact your community. This is the lever where corporate social responsibility (CSR) and reporting comes into play, but it is bigger than that. Give back and support causes that improve the world around you. The causes you back say a lot about your company. Currently, sustainability efforts are at the heart of many responsible citizenship initiatives, but this lever is essentially about showing what specific and distinctive aspects of society you care about above and beyond your own products and profits. It's about doing the right thing for the right reason, not because a nongovernmental organization (NGO) or their manifesto says so.

FERRERO

Beauty is in the eye of the beholder, so ranking responsible citizenship initiatives is difficult to do, but one that is generally regarded as very positive is the work of Ferrero, the Italian candy company. They are recognized for a premier program, Glocal Care. What I like about the program is the simplicity of it. It focuses on people and the planet. They acknowledge their interest in sharing value to create value, so they're extremely clear about the economic return. But they keep their focal point on two main areas, and they don't make it overly complicated.

6. LEADERSHIP HUMILITY

CEOs with vision, passion, and demonstrated humility in

the service of the firm make the difference in outstanding companies. The greatest organizations have dynamic, visionary leaders who also see themselves as servants. They serve their customers and their team. This quality describes not just leaders' visibility and ideas, but their attitudes, character, and the way they carry themselves in the world. The key trait of this lever is a view of leadership as an honor and privilege, not a burden or a chore.

HOME DEPOT

For three years, I had the privilege to work with one of the best CEOs and communications teams in America. Frank Blake and the team at Home Depot offer a clear example of leadership humility. When Blake took over as CEO in 2007, he returned the culture of Home Depot back to an inverted pyramid, with the CEO at the bottom.

Having the CEO at the bottom put managers, employees, and customers above him, with customers at the very top. It is a customer-first mentality. Blake's role as the CEO was simply to clear out and eliminate problems so that everybody else above him could meet the needs of the customers.

When Home Depot experienced a data breach in 2014, Blake's humility took the company the extra mile. Blake had announced that he was going to be retiring in August of that year, and on Labor Day, the data breach occurred. Instead of turning it over to the new guy—Blake was going to be leaving in November—he decided to own the situation. He took leadership on the data breach, allowing the incoming CEO to manage the day-to-day operations of the stores. Blake assumed responsibility, apologized publicly, was actively engaged in the war room that they had in their offices in Atlanta, and went out of his way to demonstrate that there was an error and that he was getting to the bottom of it as fast as he could. That's a perfect example of leadership humility. It was not a burden to serve. It was an honor to serve, and he continued to serve through his previously announced retirement date.

What I learned from the Home Depot team was the importance of humor and humility. They had a positive and long-term frame of mind that didn't let them take themselves too seriously.

7. PERFORMANCE AND RESULTS

Prove that you have a strong-performing company that is profitable, successful, and is responsible with resources. Financial and operational performance directly impact reputation: Your company is not going to be around if it's not performing well financially. Companies need to make sure they generate shareholder return, that they're operating efficiently, and that they are performing as well as or better than their market peers. This is the last on the list of the seven levers. It is in many cases the most important, but it cannot drive the reputation of a firm alone (Cole 2012).

Corporate reputation is a powerful driver of shareholder return. Company reputations are, as many already believe, real, present, and very substantial assets. Well-managed corporate reputations provide an important reassurance for investors and help to mitigate concerns over deteriorating corporate earnings. Reputation, therefore, is a useful leading indicator of investment risk.

Let's look at the financial performance over the past ten years of the top ten most highly admired companies as rated by Forbes. The average rate of return was 769.9%. The greatest of them, which was Apple, had a ten-year return of 779%. It goes without saying that corporate reputation is a driver of shareholder return. It's a chicken and egg problem, where companies with low economic returns have a difficult time growing reputation. Those that have high performance get a reputational bounce.

Companies that don't return significant shareholder benefit, shareholder value, have a very, very difficult time growing their reputation. Those that do excel reputationally get rewarded in a very significant way. The most admired companies have all had significant financial performance over a five-year and ten-year time horizon.

APPLE

The obvious example is Apple, a highly rated reputation company and one with a ten-year stock price increase of 920%, according to S&P Capital IQ. Which came first, their strong reputation or their strong financial performance? It's difficult to separate the two, and this reinforces my point that performance and results are very much a chicken and egg situation. Without the ability to sell products and grow a business, companies cannot invest in reputation-growing initiatives.

I will explain what companies can do when faced with this challenge later in the book.

SEEKING BALANCE

When we present the Seven Levers of Reputation Management to business leaders, they gain clarity about the things they can do to grow their reputation. It breaks down the complexities of reputation and makes it clearer. Instead of a vague concept—"Let's improve our reputation!"—they now have seven concrete areas to assess, expand, and improve. Now they can see seven areas in which to allocate investments that will make a difference to the long-term life of the company. With this level of understanding and clarity, reputation can be measured.

Two examples of multidimensional reputational growth initiatives stand out. These are Johnson & Johnson and FedEx Purple. While most companies have some sort of mission or manifesto or public articulation about who and what they want to be, these three are some of the best because of the clarity, simplicity, and wide-ranging nature of their approach.

JOHNSON & JOHNSON'S CORE CREDO

In their credo, Johnson & Johnson doesn't simply talk about one narrow thing. They talk about a comprehensive view of their responsibility to key stakeholders and their responsibility to doctors, employees, the community they live in, and their stockholders. It was crafted in 1943 and remains durable even though it was written long before anybody heard of CSR. They're very clear about the balance among all of the stakeholders. That credo is so clear that it's actually printed on a piece of granite at their headquarters.

JOHNSON & JOHNSON'S CREDO

We believe our first responsibility is to the doctors, nurses and patients, to mothers and fathers and all others who use our products and services. In meeting their needs everything we do must be of high quality. We must constantly strive to reduce our costs in order to maintain reasonable prices. Customers' orders must be serviced promptly and accurately. Our suppliers and distributors must have an opportunity to make a fair profit.

We are responsible to our employees, the men and women who work with us throughout the world. Everyone must be considered as an individual. We must respect their dignity and recognize their merit. They must have a sense of security in their jobs. Compensation must be fair and adequate, and working conditions clean, orderly, and safe. We must be mindful of ways to help our employees fulfill their family responsibilities. Employees must feel free to make suggestions and complaints. There must be equal opportunity for employment, development, and advancement for those qualified. We must provide competent management, and their actions must be just and ethical.

We are responsible to the communities in which we live and work and to the world community as well. We must be good citizens—support good works and charities and bear our fair share of taxes. We must encourage civic improvements and better health and education. We must maintain in good order the property we are privileged to use, protecting the environment and natural resources.

Our final responsibility is to our stockholders. Business must make a sound profit. We must experiment with new ideas. Research must be carried on, innovative programs developed and mistakes paid for. New equipment must be purchased, new facilities provided and new products launched. Reserves must be created to provide for adverse times. When we operate according to these principles, the stockholders should realize a fair return.

(JOHNSON & JOHNSON, 2017)

FEDEX PURPLE PROMISE

A modern example of encouraging balance is the FedEx Purple program. Their focus is on their employees and talking about a handful of shared values—people, service, innovation, integrity, responsibility, and loyalty. Each value is articulated clearly and concretely. That manifests itself into what they call the Purple Promise, which is, "I will make every FedEx experience outstanding." That means all experiences, not just one customer service experience but all experiences. Wherever you are in the supply chain or any of their corporate activities, you pay attention to the Purple Promise.

LEVERAGING THE LEVERS

Expect to demonstrate health and/or growth in each of the Seven Levers of Reputation Management if you wish to obtain credit from the public. You can create programs, practices, and policies true to your corporate culture that also reinforce the impact of each lever on public opinions and attitudes.

Companies with incredibly strong reputations shine on all seven levers. Balancing all the elements is admittedly easier in some industries than others, but it is important everywhere. Technology companies that employ knowledge workers may be at a bit of an advantage, but a lot of different companies succeed in pulling all the levers.

Being clear about your mission, purpose, and vision from the outset makes it easier for you to pull these levers over time, but even companies with battered reputations have the potential to create and change perceptions by pulling the levers. Look at Toyota. Following the recall of more than ten million vehicles in a three-year span, Toyota's reputation was damaged. In response, Toyota launched a series of campaigns focused on transparency to get their reputation back on track (Davis 2012).

Time, money, and manpower limits mean that not every company excels at all seven levers. You don't have to do everything to achieve results. Focusing on your strengths—more on identifying and assessing these in Part 2—can still have a serious impact. The Gallup Organization's StrengthsFinder initiative (Roth 2013) has shown that managers should not be focused on making the weaknesses of individuals better. They should maximize people's strengths and lean on those. You'll still need to work on your weak areas, but dedicating resources to developing your strengths is a powerful tool.

Many companies are already strong on the first lever—quality and reliability. They're used to thinking about the product. Most places strive for high-quality, reliable products. More challenging areas are often transparency and leadership humility.

Even if you are particularly strong in one area, though, don't make the mistake of investing in one lever to the detriment of others. I see this frequently with sustainability efforts. The responsible citizenship lever can appear easy to pull with a sustainability program and good CSR reporting, but it needs to be part of a holistic approach. Think of this like a boat with seven engines: you have to fire them all at the right speed and trim to move efficiently in the right direction.

I saw this mistake at many companies in the 1990s and early 2000s. A French petroleum refining company called Total, for instance, went overboard on the responsible citizenship lever, with a specific focus on sustainability. Total's missteps involved not just overindexing on sustainability and citizenship, but also outsourcing responsibility for that emphasis to NGOs and other third parties. A lot of companies tried this tactic, but the backlash was harsh, as they were seen as letting outside organizations dictate their agendas. The perception was that Total's commitment to sustainability was not fully owned and authentic.

Total made the mistake of focusing on one issue while ignoring the other six areas, which are equally important. Sustainability programs are great, but you can't rest your entire reputation on a single element. Total pulled the sustainability and citizenship lever without touching the others. A reputation is not created by one particular lever being pulled—it's the sum of perceptions of all of these levers over time.

I mention this example here because it highlights the importance of authenticity. Companies can certainly have healthy, active engagement with third parties, but they must also have a clear, independent vision of their impact on their environment and that impact's implications. From the example of Total, we see that you can't make all of your reputation program about one thing—responsible citizenship and, more specifically, sustainability—and, also, that you can't make it all about somebody else's agenda. You need to stand up and understand your impacts, and then communicate those to your employees and public authentically.

One reason companies so easily get overinvested in sustainability programs is that a strong infrastructure already exists. An industry has grown up around the topic: think tanks, universities, and activist groups all talk about it. Sustainability specifically and corporate responsibility generally have their own ecosystems and established protocols that companies can slip right into.

The other six levers don't necessarily have this, and that's why many companies get into trouble. In reality, though, all the levers are equally important. They need to be synchronized. In fact, the other six need to be running well if sustainability programs are to succeed at all.

BALANCING THE LEVERS

What can you learn from these examples? The key point is that these seven levers are the subcomponents that make up reputation, and all are initially of equal importance and can be tailored to meet the needs of your firm. Companies need to make decisions, based on their Awareness and Assessment of the marketplace, about what their true strengths and weaknesses are. They need to invest significantly in their strengths, while mitigating their weaknesses as best they can. The elements of reputation management rest on this foundation.

The process needs to be self-driven, based on what's in the

company's best interest, and not invested in other people's priorities. Talk to multiple, diverse public audiences, not just one that cares about a specific topic. Distribute attention to the seven levers equally at first. After some assessment, you can begin to shape specific programs and practices to bring about change over the long term.

CHAPTER THREE

WHO ARE THE
PLAYERS?

"You can't second-guess your audience. You can only do what you think is right. If you do that, your audience will appreciate you."

LYLE LOVETT, MUSICIAN

You know you need to listen to your audience, but who makes up that audience? Who needs to hear your message? What impact will their response have on you?

It's standard practice for corporate communications to include some sort of stakeholder mapping at the outset of any strategic planning process. You try to identify the internal and external stakeholders and figure out who the players are. Most stakeholder mapping exercises I've seen are overly complicated.

Stakeholder maps can be quite detailed, showing the corporation in the middle of a spider map with legs extending out to all interested parties. Consulting agencies love to create comprehensive stakeholder maps. I've done lots of them myself—they can be quite fancy, with different colors, shapes, and shading. This exhaustive mapping can be informative, but in my experience, decision-making fundamentally comes down to considering three groups—communities, customers, and critics.

In a critical moment, you often need a solution that allows you to generate a universal message that resonates across audiences. To get there, you need to identify your key audiences.

COMMUNITIES, CUSTOMERS, AND CRITICS

Identify your communities, customers, and critics and you will be able to simplify the stakeholder mapping process so you can concentrate on the folks who really matter to your company.

COMMUNITIES

Your communities typically get something from your enterprise. They get a job. Or tax revenue. Or visibility. They are represented by your employees and your geographical community. Trade organizations and elected officials may also support your organization.

The common thread among these groups is that they are aligned with what you have to say. Your communities have a vested interest in listening to your message; they stand to benefit from the association.

CUSTOMERS

Customers, on the other hand, stand ready to give something to your organization. The classic definition of a customer is a person or organization that buys goods or services from a store or business. They also give you credibility. If their expectations are not met, customers will either speak negatively about you or choose to not speak about you at all.

Your customers have a primary experience with your product and your brand. They're identified as a top priority in many companies; you need them to grow revenue.

Traditional marketing focuses on customers and potential customers, such as people who really love Apple products or the repeat Cadillac buyer.

CRITICS

Everyone has an opinion. Your critics are the people who express their opinions of something, whether favorable or unfavorable. You might think of criticism as only negative feedback, but criticism can also be constructive. Either way, your critics will make their opinions known, so you want to shape what they say to the outside world.

Critics include the media, NGOs, third-party activist groups, folks in a chat room, or an angry Internet mob. These people can create turmoil that impacts your customers and communities, and therefore, your bottom line.

Ignoring critics is a common mistake. You can learn a lot from your critics. Listen to what they have to say, evaluate it, and don't overreact. People can easily discount their critics and hold them at arm's-length, but that is a critical mistake that allows you to hear only half the story.

I see this avoidance approach often. In the agriculture industry, for instance, it's not unusual for companies to simply ignore the efforts of organizations like the Humane

Society of the United States and World Wildlife Fund. Walling off these critics is a mistake. Companies miss out on a real opportunity to learn something valuable from these groups. Instead of pushing the perceived opposition into a corner, companies can learn how to talk to their critics in a way that can turn some of them into supporters over time. There are some organizations that exist in direct opposition to everything your company stands for, and other than simply monitoring what they say, engagement is not worth very much. It's unlikely you will ever change the mind of single-issue organizations like PETA.

In social media expert Jay Baer's 2015 book *Hug Your Haters*, for example, he advocates embracing your customers' complaints. Baer suggests looking seriously at commentary in online groups, learning from it, and incorporating the lessons into your message.

Think of the Three C's as concentric circles. Your customers sit at the center—they're the ones who give you something via transactions. Communities come next, getting something from you when you work with them. The outer circle contains the critics. They say things to the larger world.

When I say that a company owns its brand and the public owns its reputation, it's the outer rings I'm talking about.

SIMPLIFY

I advocate simplifying the stakeholder mapping process because it helps identify the audiences that really matter. Concentrate on communities, customers, and critics and try to impress those audiences. The way these groups perceive your company affects how your reputation grows.

Harley-Davidson, for example, had a very complex communication stakeholder map at one time. They identified all of the different communications they were having with every stakeholder. The plan was very detailed, including not just customers, but employees, suppliers, vendors, and many other groups.

Because of that overly complex methodology, Harley-Davidson lost its way for a time. The company was trying to be too many things to too many people. When they simplified the process, they realized they needed to focus on the traditional American motorcyclist culture they had come from. When they homed in on this one concept, they resurrected the sense of freedom and rebellion that made them an iconic brand.

Harley-Davidson's CSR programs prioritize stakeholder groups as follows, arranged according to significance:

1. Customers
2. Communities
3. Environmentalists
4. Suppliers
5. Employees

They didn't have to be all things to all people; they just had to concentrate on the people who mattered—the riders. And that spirit pulled through on their nonbrand efforts. For example, the Harley-Davidson Foundation works with charitable organizations to improve education and health. In addition, the company's Supplier Diversity policy supports minority-owned and female-owned suppliers.

Having complicated systems can lead to a muddled message. Simplifying with the Three C's gives you an organizing framework that supports faster decisions during critical moments and a consistent message as you grow your reputation.

INFLUENCERS AND VALIDATORS

Much like the risk framework mentioned in Chapter 1 allows you to organize risks into categories—strategic, preventable, and external—the Three C's helps you organize your message. Within each of your audience groups, you can further refine your focus to consider the impact of influencers and validators.

Certain voices—influencers and validators—have a disproportionate impact. Recognizing them won't fundamentally change your message, but it can help you understand how to reach out to them to encourage them to amplify their voices to your benefit as well as offset those voices that seek to criticize your offerings.

Classic stakeholder maps might talk in a general way about employees in Georgia and suppliers in Germany, but you might see greater results if you concentrate your efforts on a particular person or group of people with your key messages.

Once you determine the influencer voices that have an impact, you can use social media and the Internet to track their voice and reach.

PRODUCT AND POLICY

Most companies give great thought and consideration to a new product rollout. They understand they can't afford to bring out a new product without thoughtful deliberation. There's almost always an exhaustive process in place to assure no stone is left unturned.

It doesn't really matter what the product is—a pair of glasses, a ballpoint pen, a new photocopier, or a SaaS solution in the tax industry—companies follow procedures to ensure that their investment is sound. Leaders know there will be significant consequences if anything goes wrong in the product cycle, from manufacturing to advertising.

Often companies fail to apply the same consideration to rolling out their reputation management messaging as they do to launching a product. Many companies simply make an announcement or launch an initiative, without adequate preparation. Doing so violates a basic premise about reputation management—it has to be very authentic and over time. Your reputation message must come from a place deep within your corporate DNA; it cannot be manufactured and launched separately from your company's identity and values. It cannot be mimicked from your agency's great idea for another client.

An unfortunate example of this is Maple Leaf Foods. On June 6, 2017, Maple Leaf Foods announced it had a very ambitious plan to become the most sustainable protein company on Earth. Their press release put forth "a sweeping set of principles and an expansive sustainability agenda that has yielded substantial advancements in nutrition and environmental impact, elevated animals' care, and step-changed the company's investment in social change" (Maple Leaf Foods 2017). It sounds great. Unfortunately, Maple Leaf didn't follow up with the kind of methods they would use to roll out a new product. The announcement didn't get any traction. Issuing a press release is not enough. To get the desired impact, it would require a comprehensive program and messaging.

Why don't we think about introducing a policy with the same rigor we use to introduce a product? If we agree that reputation is a critical imperative and a driver of company growth, why don't we think discipline is critical when developing and publicizing policies?

I frequently challenge clients to apply a deeper process to their reputation management efforts, much like they apply to products. Let's look at that process more closely.

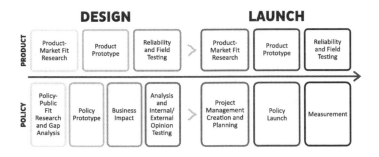

First, whether you're bringing out an iPhone or a pair of sunglasses, you need to assess whether the product meets the needs of the market. Is there a product-market fit? To find out, you'll do research to evaluate the marketplace and understand the problem solved by your product.

Next, you'll create a prototype. You'll make sample sunglasses, show them to designers, and probably do some reliability and field testing. You might get feedback from focus groups who try out the new glasses. You'll ask them lots of questions. Do the glasses meet their expectations? Do they seem durable? Useful?

By the time you even approach scaling, developing, and manufacturing the product, you'll have all sorts of information to inform your next steps.

When you finally hit the product launch phase, which is in itself a huge exercise in marketing and promotion, you'll have tools to measure your success. You can go back and look at how well the product is working for your company and consider how you can improve the process. Thus, your product quality continually improves.

What would this process look like if we applied it to policies? Policies can have significant effects on a company's reputation. Examples include Cargill announcing it would reduce antibiotics in their beef, McDonald's launching new labor practices, or the College Board announcing new policies for granting testing accommodations for students with disabilities. People take note of these initiatives; they should be as considered and deliberate as any product announcement.

Like products, policies need to first be examined for public market fit—how does the proposed policy solve a problem in the marketplace? How is it going to impact the organization and those around it?

After the gap analysis, you can create a policy prototype and play out the possibilities. What is likely to happen if we decide to raise wages, change our overtime policy, or only use solar panels? How will those decisions impact the business?

Next, you test the policy internally and externally. Get your stakeholders involved and make sure you've considered all of the implications. This is where the Three C's come in. Find out if you've considered the needs of your community, customers, and critics before you launch your new policy.

When you announce the policy, you can use traditional public relations and promotional activities. Don't forget to measure the outcome. Did you achieve the reputational impact you were hoping for?

If the things your company does have a significant impact on the way people perceive you, you should apply the same rigorous process to developing policies that you use for products. You wouldn't just jump out there with a product, nor should you with policies. You need to use a similarly thoughtful level of discernment when bringing new processes and policies to life.

Many companies today are tempted to float ideas on social media and respond to the feedback there, rather than contemplating the company's deeply-held values. If our agenda is to improve reputation over the long term, however, we can't use tactics like this. We need to make it clear that we take what we say as seriously as what we make.

UNOBVIOUS INFLUENCERS

There are, however, voices on social media you need to identify and pay attention to. The louder voices are easy to identify—people with large Twitter followings, people with thousands of Facebook friends—but the challenge is to find the niche groups. Effective marketers think about the promotion necessary to get these unobvious influencers on board.

You name the topic, and there is a community out there that talks about it. It could be animal welfare, or it could be bitcoin. It doesn't matter. Whatever the subject, there is a group of passionate people who love to talk about it.

For example, I'm passionate about sailing, and one of the blogs I read is *Sailing Anarchy*. It's about competitive racing at a local and international level. There's a contributor—user name Governail—who talks knowledgeably about small boat racing. In particular, he's interested in rules that keep the mass public from participating. His is a subcommunity in a subcommunity, but in that space, he's an important influencer. His point of view moves and drives conversations about the future of the sport.

It takes a little bit more work to identify unobvious influencers. These are smaller groups, but they're full of passionate, topic-literate people. If you want to understand the voice of your community, listen to these people. If you want your audience to understand you, craft your message to answer the questions these niche communities have.

Kim Kardashian is not going to move your reputation. It's passionate people, with passionate opinions that will. Finding them can be a challenge, but it's one that pays off.

CHAPTER FOUR

—————

HOW DID WE GET HERE?

"The 4 P's model of marketing is still king."

PHILIP KOTLER, THE FATHER OF MODERN MARKETING

Many conversations I had with CEOs and CCOs in the past came out of a crisis. Once the crisis had passed, these executives started to talk about reputation. They knew they had work to do on the reputation front, so they asked me to tell them what to do.

I happily obliged but found that as we got into the nuts and bolts of reputation management, our conversations floundered. I wondered why the concepts I was presenting were met with looks of confusion or blank stares. I realized there was a disconnect between their brand-based, marketing mindset and my definition of reputation management. Their framework and orientation was around marketing. They understood brand. They weren't too sure where I was going with reputation.

To solve this puzzle, I researched the fundamental underpinnings of marketing as a means to understand where the traditional marketing-trained CEOs and CCOs were coming from. On this journey, I learned about Neil Borden, who articulated the strategy of a "marketing mix" in the 1950s. Borden created a list of twelve policy areas managers needed to be concerned about in their marketing mix (Borden 1957).

I also learned about professor Jerome McCarthy, who refined Borden's ideas with the Four P's. The Four P's—Price, Product, Placement, and Promotion—offered a model for managing the marketing mix (McCarthy 1960). Organizing their work into these four categories helped marketers control the process. Marketing managers now had a framework for hiring, training, and managing employees as well as tasking specific outside agency partners on how to handle each of these four elements.

For the first time, marketing organizations and departments had a robust definition of their work. Previously, marketing was a little-understood discipline, sort of a second cousin to sales. Everybody understood sales, the process of getting a product in front of a customer and convincing them to purchase it. Salespeople went door-to-door selling products and services. They went to the customer. Academics like Borden and McCarthy recognized that it didn't have to be that way. Simply talking about the features and benefits of a product could bring the customers to them.

Imagine a corporate boardroom before Borden and McCarthy's ideas went mainstream. How do you suppose the idea for the Macy's Thanksgiving Day Parade was received in the 1920s? It probably sounded like a crazy idea that couldn't possibly drive sales. Similarly, how could a bicycle race—the *Tour de France*—possibly help a failing newspaper (*L'Auto*, ancestor of the current daily, *L'Équipe*)? In both cases, it worked. Before Borden and McCarthy, there was little understanding of how marketing efforts could boost sales.

By studying the Four P's, however, managers finally found a vocabulary for talking about this new field—marketing. The new framework illuminated the field of marketing and, in turn, expanded the possibilities for sales.

Just as marketers needed a new way to talk and think

about marketing, today's communicators need a new way to talk and think about reputation. The disciplines overlap, but until now, leaders haven't had a robust framework for understanding and communicating the importance of reputation. In today's boardroom, a certain amount of attention may be given to reputation, but it seldom goes very deep. CEOs know reputation matters, or have seen others in their industry get their reputation crushed, but few fully understand what it means or how to assign responsibility for it. Just like there wasn't always a common language around marketing, today we lack a shared vocabulary around reputation.

The conversation today lacks specificity. People say, "Yes, let's do some of that reputation stuff. It's good for us." Reputation seems like such an intangible asset that they often don't know where to start. It's tempting to take a laissez-faire approach. That doesn't work. You can't just do good and hope the rest will take care of itself. The Four A's that I'll cover in detail in the second half of this book will help you define what to do and when to do it.

From their experience with crises and critical moments, most leaders know that promoting and protecting their reputation is crucial. Until now, however, they couldn't necessarily see a clear path toward creating an effective reputation management program. Using the Four A's, however, leaders can access a management paradigm that supports strategic and thoughtful reputation building. The Four A's are completely actionable, giving leaders a concrete way to assign tasks and responsibilities for each element of their reputation strategy as well as the discipline to not jump ahead to inefficient actions and PR for the sake of activity. Managing your reputation is about the outcome and impact of your actions over the long term. This mindset is the key to unlock the power of reputation.

NEW LOCK, NEW KEY

The Four P's of marketing unlocked the mystery around marketing. The principles opened up an industry that has thrived and grown into healthy, dynamic systems in most companies. The lock they were opening was the power of brand and the power of the products and services of the companies that make up those brands.

Today, we're looking for a new key to unlock a new mystery—reputation. We need a manageable, concrete tool to unlock public perception around organizations. Yet, we continue to try the old key in the new lock. The marketing key won't work in the reputation lock because reputation is a different sort of beast. Where marketers focus on brand, a lock they have complete control over, reputation management needs to focus on reputation, a lock that's controlled by the public.

THE FOUR A'S

So, what does the new lock—reputation—look like? How do we open it? Enter the Four A's—Awareness, Assessment, Authority, and Action.

Just as the Four P's helped marketers organize their go-to-market efforts, the Four A's make the journey to reputational excellence manageable. Reputation is different from sales; it's an intangible asset that must be managed differently. Nonetheless, reputation can be managed.

Until now, many people's thoughts around reputation have been vague. I often hear people express excellent ideas—they want to do something for their employees, or they want to get the word out about their innovative processes—but they don't know how to implement them. The Four A's offer a measurable, sustainable mechanism for creating positive impressions on key stakeholders. The Four A's allow managers to utilize the key elements of reputation management in a finite number of logical dimensions—the Seven Levers of Reputation Management outlined in Chapter 2.

For the first time, leaders can visualize the individual elements of reputation management and articulate how they work together. If you picture reputation as a pyramid, you can see what needs to be put solidly in place on the lower levels for you to be able to reach the peak.

Kith's Reputation Excellence Model

Business leaders understandably want to reach the apex of the pyramid, the nirvana of reputational excellence. The peak experience doesn't happen all at once; it's a journey. Like a spiritual journey, you need to start with the basics, with a beginner's inquiring mind. Then you must prepare the way before you can access a higher level of growth and development.

The Four A's logically stack on each other from Awareness to Assessment to Authority to Action. This stacking creates a pathway, or process, that managers and those interested in managing reputation need to follow. The journey begins with understanding your situation. Only then can you take meaningful measurements and acquire the authority to act.

You'll see on the pyramid a heavy blue line separating the Action element from all the others. The line doesn't mark a pause in the process but a barrier that should not be crossed until the initial steps on the journey are addressed. Too often, people in pursuit of reputation management jump right into the Action phase. They jump over that solid blue line and launch activities before they have gone through the processes of Awareness, Assessment, and Authority. The Action phase can be exhilarating, but it can also eat up significant time and resources with very little outcome if those involved don't know what their targets are because they've not done the preparatory work. It can create misalignment with internal and external stakeholders and fail to meet their expectations.

Public relations activities that drive action for the sake of action are bad for reputation management. Many agencies want to push people into creating content or programs, but if there's been no underlying process, any success will be short-lived and not impact reputation over the long term. Reputation management is the long game, not a great piece of content, town hall, or executive speech.

I draw a parallel between corporate and personal development here. Say you want to bench press your body weight or finish a marathon. You can't automatically jump up to the heaviest plates or run a full 26.2 miles right away. You need to slowly increase the weight you're lifting or the distance you're running.

Some changes in life are amenable to the cold turkey change method, but transformations last longer if they're based in incremental, step-by-step adjustments. Once you've built up stamina and integrated your new habits into your lifestyle, you can bring your boldest visions to life and keep them alive.

I have run two marathons. I did one with a team that did regimented training; this group of people kept me very accountable, and I met my goal time. Preparation for the second race was a little bit more ad hoc. I thought, "I'm reasonably fit. I can go do this." On the last hill of the last few miles, I realized that I really should've trained with the team and completed those hill workouts. I had a very poor experience. The structured format of training made a difference.

The next four chapters will explain a structure for reputation management—the Four A's—in detail. For now, here's an overview:

THE FOUR A'S: OVERVIEW

Awareness, at the base of the pyramid, asks you to think about your need and desire for change.

Assessment requires you to consider the ways you might go about making the change.

Authority means giving yourself permission and the tools necessary to bring about the change you've chosen to pursue.

Action is the final step, when you bring to life the sustaining, long-term change you've been working toward.

There's really no getting around it; you have to work through this list to get to the top. The top is never the end of the journey anyway. The journey to reputational excellence actually doesn't have an endpoint; there's always more work to be done and another pyramid to scale.

PART 2

THE KEY: THE FOUR A'S OF REPUTATION MANAGEMENT

Kith's Reputation Excellence Model

CHAPTER FIVE

—————

AWARENESS

"The awareness of our own
strength makes us modest."

PAUL CÉZANNE, FRENCH ARTIST

Awareness, then, comes first. It often comes on the heels of a critical moment. Catastrophe has already struck, or you receive information that makes you realize a metaphorical fire is possible, even eminent. Maybe a competitor has run into problems you desperately want to avoid. In that moment, you become aware of the need to do something different. You need to strengthen your reputation. But what do you need to know to begin?

You'd like to know everything. However, because of the human mind's limited cognitive capacity, you have to pick the things that matter. Even if you could consume everything, you couldn't react to it because you're limited by your team's output capacity. Awareness is the process used to identify, evaluate, and monitor issues, threats, and opportunities that can harm your reputation and/or can grow your reputation. If reputation is a series of impressions that people have about a company over time, you need to create a system that allows you to be aware of the reputation-shaping touchpoints along the way. You need a system that keeps you up on what the public is saying, and that helps you differentiate smoke from fire, so you know which things matter and which don't.

Awareness is multifaceted. Internal awareness requires you, your managers, and other leaders to be aware of what's going on inside your organization. Internal awareness isn't solely developed through familiar tools like employee surveys. You gain these insights by paying attention. Walk around and talk to people. Read what your employees are saying on Glassdoor.com, and know what's happening day-to-day inside your company. Managers should have systems in place to ensure that these things happen.

External awareness means observing what's happening in the marketplace, among your competitors, and in your communities. The best leaders are inherently curious, and seek out information about the world around them. You might observe how a competitor deals with a major data breach, for instance. Other threats might be subtler, so keep your ear to the ground for news of things like political negotiations that might lead to business losses. Do you have an early warning system in place to alert you if and when these things happen?

Stick your head up and look around and understand what's going on inside and outside your company by truly looking and listening to what's happening.

SITUATIONAL INTELLIGENCE

Several concrete elements make up any good Awareness program. The first is situational intelligence. Situational intelligence describes how you manage and process all of the information you become aware of. You need to integrate the information before you make plans and take actions.

Think of how stockbrokers operate. Stockbrokers are aware of many different intelligence sources; different analysts weigh in on the equities market, the debt market, and the bond market. To recommend action, your stockbroker can't just turn the ticker tape over to you; he or she needs to analyze and improve the information and apply judgment to present it appropriately. Specifically, to make, buy, sell, or hold recommendations. Equities analysts, and by proxy, stockbrokers, make recommendations about a specific company. Do I buy it? Do I sell it? Or do I hold it? This book is certainly not about buying stocks—*Coletti* is Italian for "bad at making money in the stock market."

However, I saw this method in action and thought, how can we apply this to situational intelligence? How can we take our understanding about a particular situation and use that as a proxy for a company, to make recommendations about when to act, monitor, or back-burner certain issues?

Situational intelligence lets you look out over the landscape of the issues, see the situations that are impacting your organization or your industry, and evaluate them. You could just gather a stack of news clippings, but that does little good until you improve it by analyzing it. Using your expertise, you can identify the emerging trends that require action and recommend the appropriate response: act now, do some more passive monitoring, or simply keep the issue in mind without doing anything about it yet.

MEDIA MONITORING

Reputation management, similarly, involves synthesizing

and organizing a wide range of possibly influential information. Some data require quick action, other information might invite passive monitoring, and some items can go on the back burner to think about later. We use these three categories—act, monitor, and back burner—to help companies differentiate smoke from fire.

Corporations have always wanted to be aware of what the media is saying about them, but information-gathering methods have changed significantly over three generations.

The first generation of media monitoring, which is how I started in my career, looked like this: We got in before anyone else each day, took an X-ACTO knife and cut out newspaper articles, pasted them onto 8.5- by 11-inch sheets of paper, and made a stack of photocopies. Then those photocopies were delivered to executives' desks early in the morning so that when they came in, they could thumb through, depending on the day, a half-inch to a two-inch stack of clips. In those days, just getting on the clip recipient list was a big deal because it meant you were important and a decision maker.

Years later, in media monitoring 2.0, we started gathering those clips electronically and began to distribute the information more democratically, making everyone—not just decision-makers—smarter. Google alerts and some of the excellent media monitoring software out there make it easy. We use a program called TrendKite. There's another called Meltwater. Cision is also a popular choice. Several solid technologies can deliver information to your desktop digitally. In the simplest scenario, you can set up a Google alert for the name of your company, and you'll receive notice of every mention Google sees.

Now we're into media monitoring 3.0. That means taking that volume of information; understanding who you are; understanding the threats, risks, and issues we've talked about previously; and then having humans analyze that information much like stockbrokers and analysts do. Today, we're giving executives less volume of information but more actionable information. They can glean relevant information and make decisions on the basis of our analysis.

To do that, we need to understand the issues and recognize the trends that cause concern. That helps create a filter. Instead of thinking, "I'm interested in McDonald's," or "I'm interested in ground beef," you can specify precisely what you're looking for that relates to those two topics.

At Kith, we do bimonthly and quarterly deep dives for our clients that take all this inbound information and apply it to a particular industry or a particular set of topics within an industry. For example, we might be looking at issues related to antibiotics and food safety. We gather and organize this information to deliver situational intelligence—specific recommendations for change—to our clients.

Information can give you an early warning signal that this topic is getting more attention and new influencers and can reveal the type of influencers and the volume of media coverage. Situational intelligence, version 3.0, makes companies better, smarter, and more emergent over time. It helps you avoid getting laser-locked on topics you already know a great deal about. Instead, you can use media monitoring technology to identify emerging trends and hot spots.

A major agribusiness corporation implemented a situational intelligence program as the subject of antibiotic use in livestock production and its impact on red meat consumption was heating up. After putting the program in place, it became increasingly clear that the conversations around the topic were calling for leadership to give a voice to the manufacturing side of the supply chain, not just the end-user side.

Using situational intelligence allowed the company time

to determine the best course of action to take and when to take it. Consequently, the company announced a new policy on antibiotic use in livestock, which led to favorable media coverage in leading national newspapers, as well as industry praise.

INFLUENCER MARKETING

By 2016, your communications plan was considered incomplete if it didn't include influencer marketing, which speaks directly to two components of the Four A's—Awareness and Action. Awareness, because it requires you to take note of what influential voices are saying about you and your interests, and Action because it requires engagement with influencers.

Influencer marketing is expected to continue its growth. The new frontier of influencer marketing won't be led by bloggers pushing the latest skincare product or mobile game. Instead, companies will seek out policy influencers—those with the deep knowledge and genuine interest in learning more about a company's inner workings and policy decisions. Paid influencers will lose relevance, and the less obvious policy bloggers will emerge as the new company torch bearers.

The recent growth of paid influencer marketing, combined with increasingly strict guidelines from the FTC, means your target consumer is flooded with content often followed by an asterisk or a disclosure that the article they just read was actually sponsored content. Not all consumers are okay with that.

IS SPONSORED CONTENT DECEIVING?

A 2016 study by Contently, The Tow-Knight Center for Entrepreneurial Journalism at CUNY and Radius Global Market Research revealed that more than half (54 percent) of respondents felt deceived after reading a post, only to discover at the end of the article that it was sponsored content (Lazauskas 2016).

Beyond lacking in credibility, sponsored content from paid influencers lacks authenticity. Consumers are often left wondering if an influencer really believes in the company they're talking about, or if they're just trying to cash a paycheck. Given this increasingly challenging influencer landscape, I'm proposing a new way of finding respected policy influencers that will authentically amplify your message.

OBVIOUS INFLUENCERS

Obvious influencers are well-known. They are the significant voices in traditional and social media with the potential to drive your company's agenda. These personalities have the ability to change conversations, but everyone is already listening to them. Your competitors hear the same information from obvious influencers that you do. It's on the evening news. You need to be aware of these sources, but they're not the richest source of information.

Unobvious influencers, on the other hand, don't necessarily have a huge following on social media. These people might have 500 to 1,500 Twitter followers, but those followers are from a very specific community. They share a common interest and trade expert opinions about their topic of choice. These unobvious influencers help you do two things. First, they aid in your situational intelligence because they are typically the canary in a coal mine, the early warning signal when something is going wrong. Second, unobvious influencers are easier to work with. You can reach out to them and engage with them. Their opinions are more authentic, and they haven't been picked over by every other company out there. These folks are less apt to have a jaded view of their field. They're curious and eager to share.

Influence is not accurately measured by retweets or followers. When you only take retweets or followers into consideration, the influencers you find will always be the same people. This method is restrictive. It measures influence independent of the topic or issue. Do you want Katy Perry talking about your innovative supply chain management? Would that ring authentic to the consumers you're trying to reach? Probably not. Even when you get to a top influencer who speaks to your industry's issues, chances are your competitor will contact them, too, resulting in a bidding war in which the only winner is the influencer's bank account.

UNOBVIOUS INFLUENCERS

The best way to get high quality intelligence is to look where others are not. We try to look at unobvious influencers, influential but small voices out of the mainstream, so we can learn from them and see trends before they significantly impact a company or an industry.

Unobvious influencers are those that align with your organization's philosophy and mission but don't necessarily have the highest follower count. They have an expressed interest in your issues and understand its complexities. Unlike paid influencers, who are usually promoting a product, unobvious influencers promote your company's policies, practices, and procedures with a credible voice of support, which pulls a number of your Levers of Reputation Management.

For example, an unobvious influencer's vocal support of

your company's volunteerism at the local food bank will pull the Responsible Citizen lever, while the endorsement of your CEO's generosity to his or her employees will pull the Leadership Privilege lever. Unobvious influencers are hard to find because the current way organizations find influencers is by using obvious metrics like follower counts and keywords. This is a flawed approach.

We're making the case for targeting people who don't have a million followers but are really passionate and knowledgeable about what they're doing.

So how do we find these elusive "unobvious influencers?" Through really cool technology. Kith uses a tool called Pathar Dunami. Dunami uses heuristics—shortcuts—in social media monitoring and network analysis to determine who's worthy of following and who's not. The software identifies things like gender, geography, and communication platform. It can put people into "pro" and "con" buckets using artificial intelligence. It's quite reliable, but it's not perfect; you still need some human analysis to evaluate things like originality of content, novelty of content, and possible third-party input. Dunami helps you navigate social media and other big data sources to figure out who and what really matters. We apply the obvious targets identified on social media by keyword, volumetrics, and sentiment, then refine and expand further using military intelligence-born network algorithms and analytics.

Once you've found the right people, take the time to understand who they are and what makes them tick. Armed with these deep insights into your unobvious influencers, you're empowered to engage with the right people. By utilizing this technology, you can augment the programs you already have in place and grow in influence with voices that are not picked over, cynical, or looking for a pay-to-play payday.

Approach an influencer like you would a friend. Before you launch a new policy, call them in to get their thoughts. It makes them feel important, and it gives you a temperature check. You get a preview of how your policy is going to be received by consumers who are really familiar with whatever you're trying to do.

ACCESS AS CURRENCY

Am I suggesting you find influencers who are willing to work for free? Not at all. You're still paying unobvious influencers, just with a different type of currency, of which there are two types. The first is, of course, money. You can pay an influencer, and in return, they promote your company or idea on the Internet. But what I am advocating for is another type of currency: access and information.

With access as currency, influencers are given special access to your company's plans, policies, and procedures. In many cases, they're invited to provide input and feedback. This level of access is something money can't buy. With access as currency, you are building relationships with influencers for the long term. These influencers become interested and invested in your company and the things it does. This lends authenticity and credibility to the influencer—their audience knows they're not just in it for the money. That authenticity is reflected in the type of content the influencer shares about your company.

Once you've granted access to the influencer, it's important that you nurture the relationship. Your relationship with an influencer is not all that different from a friendship or romantic relationship. Your relationship with your influencer requires ongoing work, mutual understanding, and authentic communication, if you want it to last.

INFLUENCER IMPACT

A lot of people don't take unobvious influencers seriously, but they offer an excellent opportunity to expand your awareness. We've repeatedly seen examples of how these unobvious influencers that started out relatively small went on to have a disproportionate impact.

A classic example of this is a woman named Bettina Siegel and her blog *The Lunch Tray*, which covered issues related to school health and nutrition programs, particularly in her hometown of Houston. In a blog post, Siegel expressed outrage about Houston-area schools using "pink slime," a pejorative term used to describe a form of ground beef, in their school lunches. Siegel created an online petition, which garnered a quarter of a million signatures and support from members of Congress. After Siegel posted, the blog and her comments on pink slime spread like wildfire, leading to outraged parents and even an ABC News report. Siegel hadn't been on anyone's radar before that moment, but her blog on pink slime attracted significant media attention and caused a reputation headache for those in the beef industry. Finding people like Siegel and understanding them is a critical part of any Awareness program.

Of course, some online personalities have become savvy and may court companies seeking a sponsorship. It's even more critical, then, that your analysis team observes their content over the long term. One of the benefits of following small, unobvious influencers is that you can identify them before they have crossed the pay-to-play threshold.

Having a sophisticated process for gathering situational intelligence is more important now than ever because there's so much information to sort through. You need to understand the context of incoming information (just because it's "blowing up on Twitter" doesn't mean it's valuable) and evaluate its validity (it could be fake news you don't want to follow at all). An experienced analytical team can help you make these distinctions. Analysts are excellent at discerning general credibility and overall value.

AWARENESS AND CRISIS READINESS

To make the analyzed information you gather truly useful, you need to communicate it clearly. The landscape of corporate communications can be broken down into two types of communicators: good communicators and great strategic communicators. Let's look at good communicators first.

GOOD COMMUNICATORS

There are communications departments across the world where there are good, competent communicators. Good communicators can effectively manage typical day-to-day communications. They can handle normal activities they've seen repeatedly in their jobs and throughout their careers. Good communicators understand the tactics for moving messages to key audiences.

GREAT STRATEGIC COMMUNICATORS

Great strategic communicators have the ability to see around corners. They see interesting opportunities in everyday activities. They know how to make these opportunities innovative and exciting—to benefit their organization and grow its reputation. Strategic communicators also have the experience to know what works in different situations, and they have the boldness to accomplish their goals. As you can see, there's a clear gap between good communicators and strategic communicators.

CLOSING THE GAP: PERFECTING INFORMATION

In a crisis, it is critical that senior decision-makers get perfected information. Too often, we've been in crisis situations in which people have said, "This is going crazy on social media." That's not clear and useful information. With social media and the speed of the Internet, strategic communicators and senior leaders depend on perfected information from their team. Strategic communicators need to get good communicators up to speed as quickly as possible because information is moving so quickly, particularly in crisis situations.

So, the question remains: How can good communicators quickly accelerate their performance to be effective strategic communicators?

LEARNING PATTERN RECOGNITION

One powerful tool is the crisis simulation exercise. You do crisis simulations not to just set your team's hair on fire, freak them out, and test your systems. You do them because we know that people get better at whatever they're doing when they start to recognize patterns. Crisis simulations can accelerate learning and make your communications team stronger and better.

Fundamentally, the reason we want to make our communications teams better is to make them faster and more insightful. That happens as they develop their pattern recognition. When they see a series of shapes—square, circle, square—they know the circle's coming up next.

The key to making sure people give good information to their senior leadership team in as perfected a form as possible is to accelerate learning pattern recognition, a skill strategic communicators own.

WHAT IS PATTERN RECOGNITION?

Pattern recognition is the ability to see lasting patterns in data more clearly than other people do.

Because strategic communicators often have well-tuned pattern recognition skills, they have the experience to know that this happened and more than likely that will happen—they've been there, done that. By practicing pattern recognition, good communicators become strategic communicators because they become more comfortable and confident in crisis situations. If teams are comfortable and experienced in high-stakes situations, seeing patterns becomes easier and will yield better results.

Can anyone learn pattern recognition? Yes, absolutely. Everybody can learn pattern recognition, and everybody does learn it throughout his or her lifetime. Some of us are better than others at learning pattern recognition, but we all can learn it. But how do we accelerate pattern recognition for corporate communicators who are increasingly being put on the spot in high-pressure crisis situations?

LEARN BY DOING

You can't learn to accelerate your crisis communications performance by listening to a lecture. You can't watch a video on how to learn pattern recognition. You have to experience it and practice with it in order to gain mastery over it. I'm most excited about giving people experiential, on-the-job training in real time—it's called active learning.

That's what we do in our real-time crisis simulations. We accelerate learning pattern recognition by doing, testing, and making mistakes. We encourage group learning in a safe, concentrated environment where everyone learns from themselves and their mistakes.

What happens to communicators if pattern recognition isn't developed? Without professional development in pattern recognition, communicators develop bad habits (or they don't develop any habits). The result? They panic and don't react in the most appropriate way. If you make it through your whole career to a point of leadership and you haven't had pattern recognition experience, you fall back on what you've self-created as your own learning. In the heat of the moment, your insights and observations are weak and lack usefulness. In the worst case, senior managers won't depend on you because your insights aren't valuable—you get marginalized and put off to the side.

Learning pattern recognition does take time and money. These are resources you may not have now. But consider this...studies have quantified the cost of a crisis (Coleman 2004). Crises have an impact on brands and sales. Negative reputational events have an effect on publicly traded companies. Professional development is an investment, and there are legitimate objections to doing this type of training—but compare it with the cost of doing nothing.

In many major corporations, senior leaders who make

budget decisions view training or professional develop-ment as a luxury. They shouldn't. If they instead think about learning pattern recognition in the context of true crisis communications, they'll see it's in their best interest to have well-trained staff.

Everything is moving so fast in a crisis today that senior leaders need to make sure their team gets them the right information in the most usable way possible. That is what makes the leader most effective and useful to their boss—the CEO or board of directors.

Learning pattern recognition is the secret to capturing useful information.

PEOPLE, TIME, AND MONEY

Pattern recognition can help you manage your three finite resources: people, time, and money.

You're never going to have enough people—you'll always wish you had more. That's a given. But having out-standing pattern recognition will allow you to handle the remaining two resources more effectively: time and money.

By having excellent pattern recognition in a crisis, you

can eliminate unnecessary information that's counter-productive and slows down your responses. You save time.

Pattern recognition reduces spending on external experts because you have the expertise in-house. Very often, people in crisis have to spend an inordinate amount of money to fix self-inflicted wounds. With the expertise you've built, you'll avoid that kind of injury and save money, too.

If there is a critical moment, do you have the resources, experience, and tools at the ready to respond quickly? You know that crises are inevitable. To gain adequate awareness for an appropriate response, you need to discuss crisis readiness in your organization early and often.

Do you have a culture that allows for fast communication? Does information flow quickly? Can decisions be made on the fly? Awareness means knowing when the answer to these questions is yes and when it's no. You might find you have gaps in your processes. Exercises like crisis simulations can help you identify those. Practice for a realistic crisis—a data breach, a food recall, an executive transition, or whatever is relevant to your company—and train your company to respond. Such training increases awareness of just how ready you are, or aren't, to face a crisis.

Are you confident your team is ready to respond with the

right information to protect your hard-won reputation? Does your team have the experience and pattern recognition skills to consistently make the right decisions? Think about whether it's time to develop your good communicators into great strategic communicators.

THE CRUCIBLE OF CRISIS

I've seen many companies approach crisis planning as a purely organizational task: they accumulate endless numbers of books, binders, and checklists for various permutations of crisis. These accountings are not as useful as modeling an actual crisis situation and practicing the appropriate response. When we do crisis simulations with companies, we make the simulation as realistic as possible by creating broadcast clips and social media posts, and even have "journalists" calling in with questions to make the exercise as close to reality as possible. The participants can feel the intensity they would experience in a real-life scenario. It's an excellent test of how people communicate and make decisions internally.

We've found that this crucible of crisis doesn't develop leadership, but it reveals the leadership you have in place. Creating volumes of plans might make you feel good, and make your consultant a lot of money, but unless your people have truly begun to experience the crisis moment on their own, you don't know if you're ready or not. Simulations get everybody on their toes, reacting within a safe and healthy environment. To move forward, you first have to understand where you are today.

The people on your teams only remember 10 percent of what they read but 75 percent of what they do. The work of educator Edgar Dale (1969) on the "Cone of Learning" illustrated this breakdown.

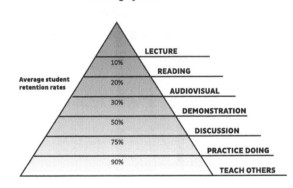

From low to high retention rates, the Cone of Learning pyramid consists of lecture, reading, audiovisual, demonstration, discussion group, practice by doing, and teaching others. Today, e-learning has advanced beyond electronic page-turning to simulation-based training. Simulation training grounds the learning objectives in a scenario so the learner can experience training as if it were a real-life situation.

The Crisis Simulator is a specialized simulator platform used to enhance learning and online dimension for crisis situations, such as a violent shooter attack, computer system data breaches, and virulent illnesses that may force company staff to react or move to a safer location.

The Crisis Simulator capitalizes on the higher levels of learning—audiovisual, discussion groups, and learning-by-doing in a virtual environment. We develop a credible crisis scenario for each company and configure a simulator platform with the right combination of social media profiles and media articles to use to deliver a response on social media platforms like Facebook, company email, and the company website.

Participants are engaged throughout the whole simulation and can role-play during the exercise. Remember, people retain 75 percent of what they do. We also include embedded video to enhance coverage of the crisis incident—according to the Cone of Learning, people remember 50 percent of what they hear and see. Team members can also monitor and respond in the Twitter-style module to incoming messages using a client profile. There are multiple Facebook timeline pages simulating the company's page where participants can post new material or respond to comments. The same capability is available in the LinkedIn-style module. We even provide custom links to download a template exercise log sheet.

Social media platforms are how companies communicate, so it's important that staff have social media tools and skills in place to manage a crisis or to even do damage control should a large-scale negative event about the company emerge.

Today, social media readiness is the mainstay for crisis communications plans. Simulations done right are a proven and effective way to learn by doing.

CHAPTER SIX

ASSESSMENT

"There is a great difference between knowing and understanding: you can know a lot about something and not really understand it."

CHARLES F. KETTERING, FOUNDER OF DELCO AND
HEAD OF RESEARCH AT GENERAL MOTORS

If Awareness involves poking your head up, looking around, and understanding the landscape, Assessment means asking, "Where do I stand with others? Where do I stand with my key stakeholders?" Assessment is the ongoing measurement of stakeholder needs, beliefs, and opinions about you.

Assessment is anchored in stakeholder research. During this phase, you're asking people for their perspective and accumulating actionable insights. Like Awareness, Assessment has internal and external components. Internal assessment might entail analyzing what your employees are saying about your company, while external research focuses on the public's opinion of your company and your competitors.

In the Assessment phase, you're considering much more than customer satisfaction with your brand. Many companies talk about reputation when they really mean brand. Clients often tell us they already have customer satisfaction data. They've asked their customers how they feel about the brand, their experience with customer service and salespeople, all things that the company can control. That's not enough.

Our mantra is "The company owns its brand, but the public owns its reputation." Customer satisfaction, for instance, is only one piece of the public puzzle. Customers who have interacted with your product may develop an understanding of what the company stands for. That's brand. In reputation management, we're looking at the opinions of a broader set of stakeholders. These people may or may not be the consumers of the particular goods or services the company sells.

The public forms an impression of the company over

the long term and over a different range of dimensions. Those dimensions can be represented by the Seven Levers of Reputation Management described in Chapter Two. Rather than asking a customer about their brand experience, a reputation manager might ask any stakeholder how they think the company is doing on the levers. Most of the levers have nothing to do with products.

Assessing how your internal and external audiences evaluate your performance across these levers gives you a clear understanding of why people believe what they believe about your business. Reputations are shaped over time and with various touchpoints; assessment is valuable because it allows you to create a baseline for measuring progress. You need to define the starting point if you are going to track improvement in any meaningful way. Looking at it this way lets you see how the actions you take change the impressions people have of your company.

Just as people sometimes overemphasize traditional media in the Assessment phase, they sometimes become overly dependent on public rankings as a source of Assessment data. Forbes, Fortune, and the Harris Corporation offer reliable reputational rankings of companies. They provide interesting information—you can see how corporations score on various dimensions—but the analysis rarely drills down to the fine level of detail you can access by investigating on your own. It's easy to get these surveys, but to achieve a level of understanding that lets you operationalize, you need to make it personal. Get a clear understanding of what people think about your specific company (and your competitors). To make solid decisions, you need information beyond the publicly available resources.

While publicly available research results are interesting, they don't necessarily measure what's important to you. They represent what's important to the surveyor, and that's not necessarily in your best interest.

What happens when you trust the public rankings too much? One cautionary tale comes from the early days of the ride-sharing service Uber. Uber was a darling of the disruptor class and enjoyed a lot of public celebration. Their early success may have blinded them to some impending problems, however. They weren't ready when a series of missteps damaged their seemingly pristine reputation. They didn't necessarily understand how quickly public perception could change.

REPUTATION RANKINGS

What information do people rely on to form their views? To cope with their bounded ability to constantly observe

myriad firm characteristics, people often rely on intermediaries to help understand and assess firms. Do reputation
rankings influence perceptions of firms? They do.

The Branding Institute (2017), a think tank based in Swit-
zerland, does a comprehensive study of all of the publicly
available rankings of reputation and evaluates their methodology and the findings of these various ranking entities,
rankings like the Forbes list of the 100 most reputable
companies in the world. There are lots of rankings out
there. Some of them are just marketing chum that somebody put together to attract attention, while others are
much more comprehensive.

The Branding Institute ranks them from top to bottom.
Forbes, Fortune, and Harris are at the top of the list.
They're highly regarded and do an excellent job. Following them are rankings by the Reputation Institute
that are equally as rigorous. After that, the quality falls
off. Some of them take such a laser-focused view on one
narrow point that the findings aren't widely applicable.
You just can't capture corporate reputation by looking at
one dimension.

People pay attention to these rankings. Michael Barnett
and Sohvi Leih (2016) did an academic study to determine
the impact these rankings had on peoples' perceptions.

Barnett and Leih told people about the characteristics of a particular company, and then either mentioned that it was highly regarded by Forbes or Fortune as one of the top fifty or top ten highly reputable firms, or they didn't mention ranking at all. Participants then rated the companies on their reputational value based on what they had just heard. Did reputation ranking influence perception about firms? Indeed, it did. Companies described along with glowing reputational rankings were rated much higher.

Barnett and Leih (2016) noted that much of the corporate reputation literature assumes people's opinions of firms are based on the actions of the firm. It turns out that people actually rely on intermediaries for their assessments. They especially rely on negative rankings, particularly when those rankings match other information they have about the firm. If, on the other hand, they already have a positive impression and the rankings confirm this, people feel even better about the company in question. These positive perceptions get reinforced over time so that companies that enjoy a reputational halo continually get a boost that makes their positive reputation perception more durable.

Without that reputational halo, it can be tough to make a mark. Walmart, for instance, has begun changing and evolving, doing work in environmental impact, but people are largely unaware of those changes. Even when people hear about these actions, it is difficult for them to bust through the old tapes playing in their heads. Reputation rankings help the rich get richer and penalize those that have reputational deficiency. The gap grows and makes it more important than ever to have robust reputation management process in place.

As has been repeated often in this book—reputation growth is a long-term commitment and not for the uncommitted. A change in perception is a long process that requires a mindset and framework that will work for the long term and be repeatable over time. A flash-in-the-pan ranking can be engineered, but true excellence is developed over time and when core values align with actions.

ORGANIZATIONAL ASSESSMENT

One of the most challenging types of assessment you must do as you create your reputation management process is the organizational assessment. Yet, it's necessary. You need to see if you have the appropriate organizational structure in place to bring about the results you want. Do you have the right people in the right roles doing the right things? Managers, absent the framework of the Four A's, have not really had a model for making a meaningful match between team members' skill sets and their roles.

Many companies, in fact, are overstaffed in media relations while they're understaffed in people who interact with influencers. Influencers directly impact your reputation over the long term—according to Bloomberg, $255 million is spent on influencer marketing every month (Weinswig 2016)—so you may need to reallocate your workforce.

An excellent example of this is the Whataburger online newsroom called What's Cookin'. The newsroom serves as a digital gathering place for Whataburger fans, customers, and journalists to keep up to date with Whataburger news, promotions, and events. These influencers are the focus, and telling stories is the key. It is a pleasure to share and create stories by both the company and the public, said Pam Cox, Whataburger VP of communications, in a press release. "What's Cookin' serves up a digital space where visitors can access all things happening at Whataburger and share their stories with us," she said.

Often, in major organizations, there's a tension between marketing and communications. Marketing is typically easier to quantify because it drives sales and you can see the impact of your marketing initiatives in your sales numbers. Communications, on the other hand, has been viewed as softer and not as quantifiable. Reputation is even further out there on the spectrum, beyond communications.

People tend to favor marketing skills because it's relatively easy to measure those results, but the skills necessary to bring true reputational change are not the same skills needed to bring a new product to market.

You need to look critically at your own organization to make sure you have a structure in place that promotes progress toward the best possible reputational results. The Four A's give you a framework for putting the right people in the right places, for allocating your resources in the most beneficial way.

CHAPTER SEVEN

AUTHORITY

"There is nothing so terrible as activity without insight."

JOHANN WOLFGANG VON GOETHE, GERMAN
POET, NOVELIST, AND PLAYWRIGHT

As you climb the pyramid, you become more aware of what's going on in your organization and begin to create specific programs—situational intelligence programs, influencer Awareness programs, crisis readiness programs, and Assessment programs. You know what's going on and you have an informed idea of what needs to change and how. But do you have the Authority to bring about significant change? Do you have permission—from company leaders, colleagues, and employees—to operationalize the insights you've gained in the Awareness and Assessment phases? Do you need permission? How do you get it?

When I was developing this model, I initially thought that gaining authority was the first step. But what good does it do to get permission if the people granting authority don't really understand what you're asking? How durable is that Authority without Awareness and Assessment to back it up? Not very durable.

To expedite the development of any project, whether it's building an office tower or a website, you need to get executive buy-in by bringing senior leaders into the project. You engage them with more than just a stated goal; you also inform them of the milestones you'll meet along the way. It's important to get authority so that you can ultimately get the budget to execute the project, but it has to be based on solid evidence. To gather that evidence, you have to do some work first.

Say Amazon wants to get into the pharmaceutical delivery business. They can't just take that idea to the leadership without testing it. They need to develop the concept—do their Awareness and Assessment—first. Then, and only then, can they appropriately seek authority. The process makes me think of a skunkworks project—where a team of engineers or project leaders goes off on their own and experiments before unveiling the results. (The term originated during World War II when the P-80 Shooting Star was designed by Lockheed's Advanced Development Projects Division in Burbank, California, under similar circumstances. A closely guarded incubator was set up in a circus tent next to a plastics factory in Burbank. The strong smells that wafted into the tent made the Lockheed R&D workers think of the foul-smelling "Skonk Works" factory in Al Capp's Li'l Abner comic strip.)

Authority seems like it's the beginning, but it seldom is. In practice, putting authority first doesn't produce great results. Senior leaders approached early in the process might say yes, but they don't necessarily understand what they are saying yes to. Even when they intuitively understand that reputation management is important, they don't always know what, exactly, they are being asked to invest in.

You can approach top management with an exciting new program and say, "Let's go! Let's do these activities!" That might pump up everyone's energy, but without a rational, logical, well-thought-out strategy, that energy will eventually wane. You have to do the groundwork first. Until everyone develops understanding through Awareness and Assessment, any authority granted has limited value.

When leaders go through this Awareness and Assessment

process, they develop a deep understanding of the risks to their reputation and the changes needed to optimally develop that reputation over the long term. Reputation management doesn't happen overnight. It requires long-term commitment. Your organization must recognize the essential need for your reputation management program. It must be embedded in the DNA of the organization if it is to carry your message consistently and effectively over time.

You can't just race to the top of the pyramid, though it's tempting. Many companies make the mistake of starting with the Action phase. The thing is, reputation growth is never a one-and-done event. Warren Buffett says it takes twenty years to build a reputation and five minutes to ruin it. If you think about reputation building over the long term, you'll do things differently.

It's an ongoing process that requires input from all parts of the organization, a deep understanding of what can go wrong, and embedded knowledge about how those events impact reputation.

RISK FRAMEWORK

Remember when we talked about the three categories of risk? When you're developing authority to act on behalf of your company's reputation, you need to be sure everyone involved comprehends the strategic, preventable, and external risks. Companies that go through the process of evaluating their risks in these categories are often rewarded with a big aha moment when high-level leaders are presented with solid evidence of what can go wrong and how it can impact the company's reputation. Suddenly, they're more than ready to get all of the appropriate stakeholders on board. Here are some guidelines to follow:

MANAGING PREVENTABLE RISKS

- There's no blaming somebody else—preventable risks simply shouldn't happen.
- Because the risk was preventable, the response should follow this protocol:
  - Focus on an apology.
  - State that the company is on top of the situation.
  - Say the company is working aggressively to solve the problem.
  - Ask stakeholders to continue to have trust in the company while the problem is fixed.

MANAGING STRATEGIC RISKS

- Understand that the public may react to your innovations and process improvements (and may view these same choices as dangerous or even as major health risks).

- Anticipate the public's reaction and concerns.
- Your first instinct should be to defend why the decision was made.
- Know that the business's reputation will be at stake, no matter which tragic event occurs.
- Empathize and understand the impacts your product, policy, or change will have on people.
- Focus on both a company's defining traits and its philosophy as an organization.

MANAGING EXTERNAL RISKS

The best response to an external risk situation is to do two things:

- Fix the problem quickly to get back to normal.
- Be part of the herd. More than likely, you are not the only firm impacted by this event.

The key takeaway is that a business doesn't need to be exhaustive with a plan for each external risk. Rather, the company needs to focus on its defining traits and business philosophy while also getting back to normal as fast as possible.

Returning to normal may require substantial expenses, but it's necessary to get up and running quickly to retain the public trust and avoid competitors stepping into the gap. In essence, the company goal in an external situation is to get back to doing what the business does best as quickly as possible, while simultaneously reminding customers that the company is simply part of the herd and not alone in facing this type of situation.

Ultimately, there's a lot at stake around the issues that pose reputational risks to a business, which is why the risk framework is not simply about how a company responds during a crisis. The framework is also about how to plan for and talk about these reputational risks in advance.

Being prepared can help prevent situations from happening that may force the company either to apologize or to fix something before it quickly impacts the business's reputation and bottom line. In addition, being prepared can smooth the way when a problem inevitably occurs. It helps to know the risks and helpful responses to them so that they can be addressed if and when the time comes.

Until that moment of clarity arrives, many leaders think everything is under control. Of course, any number of things can blow up in an organization at any given moment. That leaves organizations prone to making impulsive, reactive decisions. The risk evaluation process can buy everyone involved a little breathing room to think about the risks and consequences in a much more rational and thoughtful way.

The risk framework sets the stage for authority. How does that look in practice? One of our clients in the food industry is in the middle of the process as I write. We've arranged a series of workshops to identify possible concerns. The workshops encourage people to inventory the issues facing the organization by talking to people in operations, communications, marketing, and sales. Our goal is to help them recognize the risks from a variety of perspectives throughout the company.

Once they've identified the issues, we help them organize them into risk categories. Events they never want to happen go in the preventable bucket. Risks they can control go in the strategic bucket. Uncontrollable risks land in the external bucket. We take that framework back to all the areas of the company we consulted originally and ask them if it's accurate. Some people might say no, that they think certain risks are missing. Or they might feel that certain risks belong in a different bucket.

To see a sample Risk Management Worksheet, please visit criticalmomentsbook.com.

The feedback goes to the workshops, where we start the process of identifying programs. This process helps companies develop a framework for managing reputation management, but it's an isolated task in some ways. It has a beginning and an end.

Take our work with the College Board as an example. We talked earlier about their challenge with delivering scores to high schools in 2016. The episode had the potential to significantly impact the College Board's reputation. In late 2016, they went through the process of evaluating their potential risks. They discovered they were reacting to a wide array of events, but there were really only a handful of topics that significantly impacted them long term.

The risk-framework process illuminated the risks and helped them focus on the issues that mattered most. That allowed them to allocate resources to defend those areas because they realized they could afford to de-emphasize some other areas. It also saved them from reacting as problems came along; instead, they could put programs and procedures in place to get out in front of the most important topics.

The frameworking process sets the stage for getting the authority needed to implement the changes that need to be made.

THE REPUTATION MANAGEMENT COUNCIL

The program itself, however, will need to be managed and monitored over time. Who will do that monitoring? A Reputation Management Council. This is a body of leaders from across the organization that comes together to evaluate the risks and set an agenda for implementing programs. The responsibility for the ongoing massaging of the programs lies with this council, which can be only as effective as it is authoritative.

To create a Reputation Management Council, you need to involve people across the organization. In some organizations, the Council might be the executive leadership team. You don't always need to create a new structure. In other places, a separate Reputation Management Council works best. Either way, the group's function is to evaluate risk and grow reputation. It needs to be led within the senior levels of the organization.

The role of the Council is to take the framework they've created, evaluate the progress that's been made in mitigating the potential impact of all the preventable threats, and judge whether the strategic threats warrant a significant investment. The Council puts the programs in place and guides the reputation management activities at a strategic level. They evaluate the impact that reputation growth has on their organization. They clarify which personnel will be responsible for which tasks. They articulate roles and responsibilities.

I recommend that Councils be led by someone other than the CEO. People with operational authority in the organization are excellent candidates. So are senior leaders in communications who can talk candidly about the impact of the decisions the Council makes.

Councils look different in different organizations. Six to ten people is the ideal number of people; at this size, you can get all the major decision-makers around the table in almost any corporation. You'll want involvement from legal, operations, communications, and intellectual property staff.

Because reputation is dynamic, it has to be managed over time. The cadence and timing of a company's Reputation Management Council meetings depends on the culture of the company. Some of them meet monthly, others quarterly. Consider the type of industry you're in, your goals, and your company's capacity.

The process I've described here may sound overly complicated and time-consuming, but it doesn't need to be. In fact, we've developed a process that moves very quickly. We don't encourage the Council to micromanage every aspect of the program but to focus on the particularly thorny issues. Meetings begin with a check-in on the risk framework, followed by an opportunity for everybody to bring potential issues to the table. We do that in a rapid-fire format in which we quickly sort which issues will be pushed back out into the organization and which will be flagged for deeper discussion. After those discussions, the group creates an action plan. Those actions are reported back at the beginning of the next meeting.

Once you've done the cataloging and inventorying of your risks, an approach would be to take those three buckets to the Reputation Management Council and talk about them. Rank them, sort them, and decide what you're going to do about them. Depending on the culture of the organization, that can be a very laborious process.

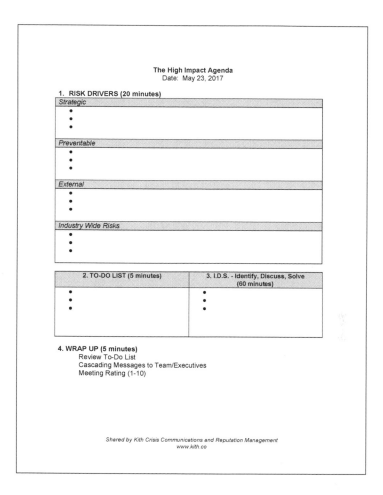

The High Impact Agenda
Date: May 23, 2017

1. RISK DRIVERS (20 minutes)

Strategic
-
-
-

Preventable
-
-
-

External
-
-
-

Industry Wide Risks
-
-
-

2. TO-DO LIST (5 minutes)	3. I.D.S. - Identify, Discuss, Solve (60 minutes)
• • •	• • •

4. WRAP UP (5 minutes)
 Review To-Do List
 Cascading Messages to Team/Executives
 Meeting Rating (1-10)

Shared by Kith Crisis Communications and Reputation Management
www.kith.co

To improve that process levering off the excellent work created by the Level 10 Meeting Agenda (EOS 2017), we've created an agenda that helps sort away small, short-term issues that can be dealt with in real time and provides space to tackle the more complex issues that you need to identify, discuss, and solve (IDS). The agenda takes the easier things and puts them on to-do lists for individuals, getting them out of the way of the more comprehensive endemic issues that touch multiple people in the organization. Those people are then free to dig into the IDS process in a more comprehensive way.

Mitigating risk is critical for crisis readiness. Having a Reputation Management Council enables you to look around corners. The High Impact Agenda maximizes productivity and accountability.

A Reputation Management Council provides an enterprise-wide view of risk and ensures an ongoing discussion is happening with the right people at the right time. The absence of a real, time-sensitive threat can cause businesses to delay planning or to not plan at all. Alternatively, trying to prepare for every scenario can be overwhelming and impractical. A Reputation Management Council meets regularly to discuss risks facing your organization and create an enterprise-wide view of risks that could impact your reputation.

We know that reputation is important—many deem their company's reputation as important as its profitability. According to the Center for Corporate Reputation Management at LeBow College of Business at Drexel University, "corporate reputation is estimated to be worth about 4 to 5 percent of sales per year. Reputation is the most valuable asset entrusted to a CEO by the Board and shareholders" (Schreiber 2017). The Center for Corporate Reputation Management at Drexel also notes that reputation builds competitive advantage: "Studies have found that organizations with better reputations do better financially, attract and keep talent at lower costs, have lower costs of capital, and more easily gain support from government and other stakeholders in times of need." (Indian River Admin. 2014) A Burson-Marsteller study (2010) found that 95 percent of chief executives surveyed believed that corporate reputation plays an important or very important role in the achievement of business objectives. Yet most organizations do not have a venue dedicated to reputation where critical thinking about reputation growth and risk could take place among key company leaders, which would lead to faster, better response. A Reputation Management Council solves that problem.

Reputation Management Councils must be cross-disciplinary. A good Reputation Management Council should have representation from Communications, Operations and Legal, at a minimum. Why do we place such an emphasis on everyone having a seat at the table? Think about the last crisis your organization had.

Too often, I see companies in crisis get bottlenecked by internal misunderstandings of chain of command. You've probably been on the receiving end of a proposed statement that had so many editing marks it looked like it was bleeding. Legal won't let the communications team say what they want to say. Government Relations is upset that they weren't able to give their stakeholders a heads up. Operations is frustrated that no one understands the complexity of what they're trying to fix, and that, no, they can't just flip a switch and make it right. This leads to slow crisis response times, which causes angry stakeholders and loss of consumer trust. Can you imagine if you had established an understanding and common vocabulary before a crisis struck, just how much easier that particular crisis would've been?

A lot can go wrong when there's not a venue to regularly discuss reputational risk. A great example is what happened with Unroll.me. It faced backlash for selling its data to Uber, who used that data to keep tabs on its competitor, Lyft. This is a completely legal practice—one that Unroll.me users agree to in the terms and conditions—but with Uber in the hot seat for its own avalanche of crises, the media and public viewed the revelation of this practice under a new, much angrier lens.

Granted, hindsight is twenty-twenty, but I believe that

Unroll.me would have been better equipped to respond to this crisis if they had a venue to discuss and prepare for this risk. To be clear, I'm not saying they would have decided to not sell their data to Uber. That was a strategic risk—a risk that a company chooses to take for significant investment return. What I am saying is that had the risk been discussed at the time of the decision-making, or even shortly after, Unroll.me's communications team would've been better prepared to respond, and maybe that blog post from the CEO that added fuel to the outrage fire would've never been published.

If I've convinced you that your company needs a Reputation Management Council, and I hope I have, you're probably wondering how to get started. Here are the basics:

CREATING A REPUTATION MANAGEMENT COUNCIL

First, gather representatives from across disciplines. As I mentioned earlier, we recommend having representatives from Communications/Marketing, Legal, and Operations, at a minimum.

Next, set a regular, recurring meeting. We recommend quarterly at a minimum. This meeting is where the group will discuss and plan for the various risks facing your organization.

Once representatives and meeting dates or frequency is determined, you'll have each of the representatives (and their respective teams) think about and compile risks presently facing the enterprise. This information will be used to populate an agenda for the Reputation Management Council Meeting.

Kith has created an agenda adapted from the Level 10 Meeting template that drives your Reputation Management Council to have a productive, efficient meeting. We call it the High Impact Agenda. This agenda is divided into four sections:

RISK DRIVERS

The first section, the Risk Drivers, is where risks facing your organization are categorized. This happens before the meeting. Each discipline will have compiled risks and added them to one of four sections: Strategic, Preventable, External, or Industry-Wide risks. When covering this section of the agenda, your group will discuss each risk and make a determination as to whether it belongs in the To-Do List section or the IDS section.

TO-DO LIST

To-Do List items are risks that can be addressed or solved

relatively quickly. If there is a Risk Driver that has a relatively straightforward solution that can be solved within the next 30 days, put it in this section. When you review the To-Do List, assign an action and owner—the person or/group who is responsible for implementing the solution. Once each item in the To-Do List section has been assigned an action and owner, you move on to the IDS section.

IDS

This section is the issues-solving track meant to create clear, actionable solutions. The IDS model is performed by Identifying the issue, Discussing the issue, and Solving the issue. Identifying the issue may mean additional exploration into the root cause of an issue, or providing additional context to uncover the real issue at hand. Discussing the issue is exactly what it sounds like—discussing the issue openly and honestly. This is the opportunity for the Council to share their group's point of view and unique challenges they face in addressing the issue. Then you solve the issue or determine next steps. Once the Council agrees on a solution, action items must be owned by someone and added to the To-Do List with the expectation that it will be completed within thirty days.

Lastly, you have your concluding items, which are to

recap the To-Do List, determine how you will cascade the information discussed during the Council meeting to your respective teams and/or executives, and rate the meeting. In rating the meeting, everybody weighs in on a scale of one to ten. This is so you can chart progress on whether the meetings are improving or declining in quality. It sounds cheesy, but we highly recommend it so that you hold yourselves accountable for making meetings productive.

We believe Reputation Management Councils are critical to an organization, so much so that it's a key piece of Kith's Model for Reputation Excellence. Clients with Reputation Management Councils have seen crises become more manageable or have avoided several crises entirely.

A Reputation Management Council will help you address crises in advance, helping you to weather the crisis storm more effectively.

CHAPTER EIGHT

ACTION

"Leadership is absolutely about inspiring action, but it is also about guarding against mis-action."

SIMON SINEK, AUTHOR AND MARKETING CONSULTANT

I know the desire to take action is incredibly strong, but let's look more closely at the reputation management pyramid.

See that bold line between Authority and Action? That heavy blue line indicates a transition process. To develop a truly clear vision, we need to take a minute to gain some perspective before jumping into action.

In more than twenty-five years of working with companies in various states of crisis and/or crisis planning, I saw

Kith's Reputation Excellence Model

companies recover from one crisis, vow to never, ever go through that again, and then jump right into an action plan. Quick changes reap cheap rewards. Corporations and their agency partners have incentive for taking action like running employee engagement programs, executive leadership positioning, and sustainability campaigns that generate positive attention. The people producing these programs get a lot of credit for nice work. It's misplaced, though, if the programs are treated as a starting point. They need to be an end step in the reputation management process, not the first.

When I started my own firm, I took time to pause, reflect, and think about what was truly necessary to make sure these companies were resilient and ready if an adverse event happened. I had done my fair share of moving people quickly into the Action phase, but I could see that approach didn't work in the long run. I came to an understanding that simply racing to the top of the pyramid, running to take action, was a mistake. I knew why people did it—to ease the uncertainty of the "Where do we go from here?" and "What can we do now?" moment—but it rarely helped. I could see that it was a strategic mistake for the company. It was a mistake for their agency partners or outside consultants—people like me—to suggest it.

It is often a disservice to corporate clients to recommend action for the sake of action. In our go-go, quarter-to-quarter thinking, there is pressure to act now. As advisors in a service business, it is hard to slow down. Some clients don't like to hear that and want immediate magic results. That is fine, and sometimes the situation dictates rapid response and programs. However, I believe if reputation formed over the long term, it is altered over the same time frame. All consultants and communications leaders should reflect on the blue line and the skip the desire to jump it too fast.

Think of times you made personal changes in your life. Maybe you decided to lose weight or get fit. You needed to work your way up to your goal; you couldn't just go out and run a marathon. That's a good way to get hurt and harm your chances of long-term success. Instead, you must go through a process of becoming aware of your problem, assessing the situation and the tools available, attaining control and authority over the situation, and finally, implementing a plan. You'll recall the product development and rollout process we talked about in Chapter 3. We have a similar vision for corporations.

READY, AIM…

In business, the Four A's we've identified set up building blocks for managers to look at their enterprise and understand it from a vision and mission standpoint, a practical and functional angle, and an external perspective. The method requires a 360-degree view of the enterprise, a DNA-level investigation of your situation and standing. With all that knowledge on board, you develop a robust vision that can grow your reputation.

The vision grows throughout the process of the Four A's. You begin seeing patterns in the initial stages of Awareness and Assessment. You identify gaps and start thinking about programs you'll want to implement, but these plans will become richer once they're strategically aligned to the risks you're trying to mitigate. As you go through this journey, you'll incorporate what you've learned into programs you already have, and you'll start looking at what needs to change to implement new programs.

Let's say, for example, you do a crisis readiness exercise and you realize you don't have relationships with critical reporters or key third-party stakeholders. You can begin working on those relationships right away and continue throughout the process. When you approach time to launch, you will have an integrated and synthesized plan and the authority to implement it. You'll also have a solid structure in place, so your actions will be sustainable over the long term, thereby growing your reputation.

Awareness identifies the problem, assessment helps you articulate the content you want to share, and authority lets you get the right people involved to sustain your efforts.

Moving up the pyramid, the greatest temptation to leap into premature action comes in the Awareness and Assessment phases. Significant learning and growth will come from these practices alone. People gain insights that make them want to act. The company can start to see the form of programs they want to put in place, and it's tempting to just do it. But without the high-level, strategic review of risk, the learning isn't integrated far enough into the organization to support long-term actions.

You can produce glossy brochures and launch sophisticated websites articulating your environmental or social programs, for instance, but a lot of times you're just checking the social responsibility/sustainability box. Without meaningful support from the senior levels of the company, your actions are perfunctory. The public will see through that. When your CEO, your board of directors, or your Reputation Management Council has a holistic understanding of the need, on the other hand, they can respond to action plans authentically, openly, and in alignment with the company's values. The public will see that, too. The biggest risk is not taking the Authority step.

Let's look at an example. In 2013 I worked with Cargill, a company that had taken a reputational hit from viral social media reports about a beef product that they and one other company in the industry produce. They realized they didn't have the appropriate situational intelligence in place; they needed better social media monitoring. They didn't necessarily understand what their stakeholders expected of them. They also needed to make sure it was okay to talk publicly about some of the risks they faced. They needed to develop their Awareness, Assessment, and Authority before making a move. They waited a year and sought to develop a program to return the product back into commerce. They intentionally waited that long to reintroduce the product. Meanwhile, they learned from customer and marketplace feedback and expanded their messaging based on price, reputational readiness, and trust.

We created a leadership platform and a leadership series at Cargill—the Cargill Leadership Series. They rolled out quarterly events featuring topics of mutual interest to the company and its customers. Each event encouraged open and transparent information-sharing. If we had launched this program right away, we might have solved the immediate problem, but we would not have addressed Cargill's reputation management needs going forward.

But Cargill walked through the progression from Awareness to Assessment to Authority. Now, they have an ongoing leadership platform dedicated to talking to stakeholders about key issues. The meetings build a level of trust and understanding, which creates a reservoir of resiliency if there is a challenge in the future. Over time, they will build up this reservoir of goodwill because they've taken the time to create, at the highest levels of the company, content and insights that are truly valuable. Instead of solving only the immediate problem, they created an evergreen program that continues to show results over time.

Finite action is critical and appropriate for brand management where there's a need for a transaction and you've got to deliver on it. Because reputation is built over time, there needs to be symmetry in the response. If the definition of reputation is that it's built over time, the solutions you propose need to be presented over time. You can't do that if you grab one particular deficiency and run with it.

ENGAGEMENT

Corporations are notoriously bad about engaging third-party advocacy groups and special interest groups. They tend to live in a self-referent ecosystem where they talk to their own employees, their trade associations, their customers, and their industry partners. Third-party engagement, though, is critical. When you've established an Awareness, you've Assessed the lay of the land, and you've developed the Authority to act, that's the time to confidently engage with third parties.

Progressive organizations that successfully create reputational resilience are the ones that invite third parties in. Asking outsiders to weigh in requires courage. Everyone likes to be comfortable, and some of those third parties are going to ask uncomfortable questions. They could even take you to task in public. Some of them may not be working with others' best interests at heart. They may take your information and spin it maliciously. That doesn't happen very often, but it's a risk. Reaching out to these parties means overcoming the fear of the unknown.

NGO ENGAGEMENT

Engagement with NGOs is no longer optional.

Consider the Army Corps of Engineer's announcement that it would halt construction on the Dakota Access Pipeline following months-long, highly visible protests by members of the Sioux tribe and their supporters. (While this construction stoppage may be temporary, it's still a significant development for all parties involved.)

At Kith, we often say that NGOs always win. In this instance, the NGO on the winning side is the Sioux tribe and its supporters. The losers are the proponents of the pipeline's construction. But the supporters of the pipeline were doomed to lose long before a single protest sign was raised.

Notice that in addition to concerns over the pipeline threatening their water supply and sacred sites, the Sioux tribe said they were not adequately consulted on the Dakota Access Pipeline project. The Standing Rock Sioux and the nonprofit Earthjustice sued the Army Corps of Engineers in federal court, arguing that the agency had wrongly approved the pipeline without adequate consultation. The protests began shortly after the lawsuit was filed.

Not engaging with the Sioux tribe effectively has proven to be a critical moment that created the current issues. Because of their failure to engage appropriately, those involved with the Dakota Access Pipeline have and will continue to face backlash from stakeholders, including consumers, government officials, and the media.

Situations like this can be neutralized, if not avoided entirely, by preparation and proactive engagement. When activists attack, the risks to your organization's reputation and even your bottom line are higher than ever—that's why it's critical to engage. Failure to engage strategically with NGOs can lead to a loss of reputation, financial turmoil, or, as those involved with the creation of the Dakota Access Pipeline, a complete derailment of business plans.

Failure to engage with NGOs caused backlash and project failure for those involved with the Dakota Access Pipeline, but the protests and subsequent negative media attention could have been neutralized or avoided entirely.

If you're really clear about who you are, understand your place in the market, and have authority from leadership to engage, you stand to benefit a lot more from these relationships than you risk. You have to overcome your fear by engaging with them over time. Organizations that engage with key stakeholders are the most successful because they can rely on people to come to their defense in a crisis and simultaneously help them broaden their message over time.

Walmart, for instance, does an excellent job of engaging with activist groups. Walmart is crystal clear about what, why, and how they do what they do. That clarity comes from work in Awareness, Assessment, and Authority. Their solid foundation allows them to listen to people's input on labor practices or product sourcing. Walmart has listened to environmental organizations and has implemented a progressive energy savings agenda because of it. It's going to take a while, but they're committed to the investment. People don't commonly know that about Walmart now, but as the program grows, it will become part of their reputation.

...FIRE

Most organizations are already implementing some actions, like building and consulting crisis response plans and hosting promotional public relations events. The kinds of actions we're talking about here at the top of the reputation management pyramid, though, come not from an internal department but from leadership.

LEADERSHIP MARKETING

The culmination of all of your work in Awareness, Assessment, and Authority creates a leadership agenda. When you market that program, you're doing what we call leadership marketing. You won't give up your brand programs or your media relations efforts, but you will take actions from the top. Day in and day out, you'll still be responsive with media relations, crisis response, or issues management. You'll also continue to do promotion around products and services. With reputation management, though, you'll add leadership marketing to the mix. Specifically, you will use the leadership agenda you've developed using the Four A's to get credit based on the Seven Levers of Reputation Management we articulated earlier. The sum of those programs is leadership marketing.

Levers to Pull for Reputation (Growth)

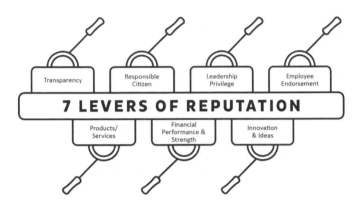

Leadership marketing takes the mindset of product development and applies it to the creation and implementation of policies that represent our leadership positions. Successful leadership marketing programs run long term, are not reactionary and are not directly related to the features and benefits of any product. They are, however, directly related to what you've learned on your journey through the Four A's.

The Four A's define your corporation's leadership positioning, and now it's time to market that leadership. Action can take many forms, but the underlying principle is that the action must be appropriate, relative to reputation growth, and sustainable over the long term.

SUCCESS STORIES

Some major enterprises that have done an excellent job with leadership marketing are American Express, GE, and IBM.

AMERICAN EXPRESS OPEN FORUM

The American Express OPEN forum, for example, launched in 2007. The forum represents one of the best visions for leadership marketing success that I've seen. First, they used nomenclature their audience understood. They were aware of their audience—small business owners seeking information on how to grow and be more successful—so they focused the content squarely on them. Then they built a new community around a group that already existed on LinkedIn. That allowed them to be hugely successful in multiple venues, but it was still clear that American Express was facilitating the conversation. They created communities that they owned but that were very open. Finally, they let outside experts share their observations on anything from insurance to HR to time management. They didn't create a walled garden that was only open to American

Express insiders. It wasn't just employees writing, but many different kinds of people.

Having that mix made the small business owners trust the forum. They knew it wasn't just a sales pitch; the forum offered actual information from real people. At the same time, American Express's sales were supported by the forum because problems identified on the forum were often organically solved by an American Express product or service. They never could have come to this approach without having a well-thought-out framework in place. On one level, the OPEN forum was a program to sell credit cards, but it has become a strategy to grow a reputation as a problem-solver specifically for small business—a core business for American Express. They pulled a number of the Seven Levers of Reputation Management with one specific program, as well as meeting their communications objectives.

GE

One of the best examples of leadership marketing or taking good works and responding to public concern is GE. The now Boston-based General Electric is often the source of public and third-party scrutiny around issues related to the environment and resource usage. The issue of climate change became the center of the bull's eye and was a significant vulnerability for the company. Beginning in 2005, the much-heralded Ecomagination Partnerships set the stage for GE to lead the way not only for itself but for their customers and suppliers. The Ecomagination strategy involves investing in cleaner technology and business innovation, developing economic growth solutions, avoiding emissions, reducing water consumption, committing to reduce the environmental impact of their operations, and developing strategic partnerships to solve some of the toughest environmental challenges. The then-CEO of GE Jeffrey Immelt stated that the work of Ecomagination was "not just good for society, it's good for GE investors." (Phyper and MacLean, 2009) It's a core part of the strategy for growth. GE used leadership marketing and savvy business partnerships with companies such as Walmart, Intel, and Statoil not only to transform their business but to also tell great stories. The Ecomagination Partnerships—a blended strategy/brand model—has evolved into an overarching idea to cover everything from operational improvement to innovation initiatives, both internal and external.

IBM

When IBM's reputation stalled and people began seeing its services as merely average, they responded with innovation around a platform, rather than a product. They took innovative technology like IBM's Watson (an artificial intelligence platform) and not only applied it to solving complex problems such as medical diagnoses and care, consumer behavior, and weather forecasting but also to more mainstream challenges like winning a game show like *Jeopardy*, designing an LED-filled dress for the Met Gala, or writing an emo song with Musician Alex Da Kid. This approach allowed IBM to revamp its reputation as a technological dinosaur and instead rebound as a source of innovation and ideas.

LEADERSHIP MARKETING AND CONTENT MARKETING

The goal of leadership marketing is not simply to sell something. The goal is to promote and grow reputation through the leadership of the company. It's distinct from content marketing, but many of the durable philosophies of content marketing apply. The basic building blocks are the same.

As early as 2001, the desire to share content in a helpful and authentic way has driven much of the thinking around public relations and communications. Companies have long used the term "content marketing" to tell stories that attract and retain customers. The reality is that growing your reputation over the long term is no different. The building blocks are the same.

The Content Marketing Institute has done an excellent

job of articulating a framework for the what and why of content marketing, and a lot of what they've outlined works in leadership marketing as well. Let's look at some of the insights we can draw from the work the Content Marketing Institute has done.

Five questions will help you define the kind of content you're going to roll out in your reputation management program. They are:

WHAT IS YOUR PURPOSE? WHAT ARE YOUR GOALS?

Think about why you want to create content. What's the value? What are you trying to share with people that is valuable to them, not just self-serving?

Your purpose comes from developing your risk framework, understanding your risks, evaluating your concerns, and defining why you are doing this. Your goal stems from what leadership has articulated about what you need to defend or what risks you need to mitigate. Your ultimate goal is to grow your reputation, especially with key audiences.

WHO IS YOUR AUDIENCE?

Who do you want to talk to? You won't know unless you've done the hard work of the Assessment phase. If you've asked good questions in the Assessment phase, you'll have a clear idea of who your audience is and your audience will have already begun to give you feedback. By answering this question, you begin to think about the people who will be hearing your story. How will they benefit from it?

WHAT IS THE STORY? WHO WILL TELL IT?

If you're going to tell your company's story, you'll need unambiguous authority from your organization and clear insights into what makes your company tick. You build content around that.

Next, consider who is best suited to deliver the story? Your CEO could be the greatest evangelist you have, or your employees might be your biggest advocates. Or, as with American Express, outside experts might be the best ones to tell your story. Your Awareness work will help you define this.

WHAT'S THE PROCESS? HOW WILL YOU CREATE CONTENT?

You've thought about the specific and unique ideas you want to share and who will share them. But how will you deliver them? Do you have a structure in place? Do you have the authority from your organization to roll out this content? Consider how you will manage the content over time. Again, you'll need to have the courage to talk to third parties about your content as you move forward.

HOW WILL YOU MEASURE ITS EFFECT?

If you've already gone through the Four A's of reputation management, you've built in a measurement function: assessment. Research is a continual and ongoing exercise.

The framework of purpose, audience, story, process, and measurement works whether you are building content, relationships, or reputation. The biggest stumbling block I see people face when they try to tackle this process is not having enough patience. Reputation is a discipline that requires long-term investment in a far-reaching vision. Because reputations are formed by long-term engagements, the process requires a strong commitment.

When the top levels of the corporation don't make such a commitment, people are tempted to jump in with the first three ideas that spring to mind, knowing that they don't have the support to sustain anything more.

That's why the discipline around understanding what moves reputation is critical. We subscribe to the belief that the levers—quality and reliability, innovation and ideas, workforce endorsement, transparency, responsible citizenship, leadership humility, and performance and results—are the best way to understand where you stand and what you can do about it. Each action you want to take goes through the filter of these levers. You always need to be asking yourself, "Which one of these levers is this action pulling?"

That keeps everyone focused on what needs to be done.

Even the best and most highly regarded, reputationally strong companies are never done. They never reach the top of the pyramid. There's no summit and then they're finished. It's an ongoing and perpetual pursuit to grow and expand your reputation over the long term. That journey has no final step; there's no last rung on the ladder. Once you start developing actions that meet the needs of specific stakeholders, you'll return once again to the Three C's and the Seven Levers of Reputation Management to address other areas of deficiency. Self-improvement builds on itself. There's always an opportunity for growth, expansion of your ideas, and who you communicate them to.

You can achieve excellence. Look at companies that are really good at reputation management—highly regarded companies like BMW, Starbucks, and Google—and you'll see that they can't stop doing what they're doing. The pressure to continue is even greater.

CONCLUSION

"How difficult it is to save the bark of reputation from the rocks of ignorance."

PETRARCH, ITALIAN RENAISSANCE SCHOLAR

This book was written to shed light on a misunderstood topic—corporate reputation. Many people are unsure about how reputation management works. But they know a good corporate citizen when they see one. Many companies don't know where they stand in society or where they stand reputationally relative to the marketplace they sell in. We want to help you avoid being unsure—unaware—of these things. Defeating this lack of awareness is one of the main building blocks of reputational management.

For example, in 2001 the Orlando Magic wanted to build

a new arena adjacent to the facility they were playing in, but they were not reputationally ready. When they came in asking for support to build the new arena, they were perceived as outsiders.

For the Magic, this was a critical moment. This moment could have set them on the path for an NBA Championship and could have reinvigorated the portion of the town where they wanted to build their new arena. To set the stage for this moment, they needed to develop a reputation as a good civic partner. They needed public support.

In the end, wishing for it wasn't enough; the initiative was not successful for a number of reasons, primarily because the team was not sufficiently invested in the marketplace. As I was in the middle of this situation, it began to dawn on me that companies can be better at growing their license to operate more successfully over time and with an end in mind. In 2001 I didn't have the vocabulary to express this as reputation building, but the vision had begun to form in my mind.

I didn't do anything about it for quite a long time, but it really dawned on me that there had to be a better way to do this for companies, basketball teams, anybody that wanted to try to grow their license to operate, wanted to expand their business and wanted to be known for something more than the last misstep they had made. It can't be just done all at once. It has to be relative to an investment over the long term.

In twenty-five years of having been engaged in some of the most significant critical moments that have shaped major corporations internationally, I realized it was not only critical moments that make or break corporations. It was how they responded to those situations in real time, and over the long term, that set the stage for the reputation that they were going to have or the reputation that they were going to build. It was on the backside of those critical moments that they needed to find a better way to grow that reputation.

Having met with CEOs, CCOs, CMOs, and other business leaders, and gotten a clear understanding of their misunderstandings, as well as their vision for the future, I started to talk about ways to make reputation management manageable. I got a lot of head nods. People agreed that was exactly what they wanted and needed.

I noticed that when the consultants left, the company had to fend for itself. The company was left without a framework or mechanism for management that communicators and marketers and CEOs could use to make sure the functions critical and proven to grow reputation were in place. Specifically, reputation lacked a framework so that communications leaders could clearly tell their team what to do and when and in what time frame. With the framework in place, reputation leaders have a toolkit that helps them assign people to focus on awareness and other people to focus on assessment, on a day-to-day basis.

I knew that marketing had been ill-defined until the arrival of the Four P's, and I could see that we needed to articulate a new set of functions for reputation management. That led to the birth of the Four A's. Without Awareness, Assessment, Authority, and Action, those companies were left to do what they thought was in their best interest based on limited feedback from select stakeholders. The concept was never truly ingrained into the DNA of the organization.

We've proven over time that this framework can empower corporations to understand reputation not only in a theoretical way, but anchored in real, practical solutions. When they harness this concept to the understanding that there are a finite number of levers they can use to impact reputation, companies can create systems for leaders, CEOs, and CCOs to truly measure, evaluate, and execute reputational programs for the long term. Before the Four A's, nobody had done that.

For the first time, we've given chief communication officers, or those who lead reputation within an organization, a model. They have a way to operationalize and manage reputation, something they've never had before. It's a liberating experience, and it creates an equivalency with other disciplines within the corporation when leaders understand that reputation management is more than simple marketing.

This framework was born out of some sort of crisis. You've had a crisis in the past, or someone in your industry has suffered a crisis you want to avoid. When you're in any of those states, you need a model to make sure you can grow your reputation in a meaningful way and improve your crisis resiliency. That's what we've created here.

The framework of the Four P's opened an old lock—that of marketing programs. It was a key that unlocked all that could happen within those elements—price, product, place, and promotion. The skill sets and expertise of the disciplines unlocked opened up an industry with a vision to make marketing rational.

Now we have a new lock called reputation. How do we unlock that? Our new key is the Four A's of reputation. They have the ability to unlock the power of reputation and make it truly manageable, taking away the confusion and mystery that's surrounded the topic for too long.

So, you may ask, is it beautiful at the top of the pyramid? I don't know, it's not that simple.

As a society, we are bombarded with specific vision of beauty. Beauty is defined for us by the images we see in the media, so that's what we think represents beauty. Similarly, reputation is judged by various entities who tell us what is good and bad. I encourage readers, instead, to develop their own view of reputation, much as you have your own view of beauty. What is right for you and the stakeholders you truly care about?

The reputation of your company is what allows your organization to be an active participant in society; our corporations play a critically important role in the growth and evolution of our culture. Your reputation should be unique to you and very authentic. Much as you define beauty for yourself, you can define reputation.

An authentically developed reputation not only improves your resiliency but also your ability to operate and thrive over the long term. When your corporation enjoys a healthy reputation, it can become a vital long-term par-ticipant that's actively engaged with society and grows in ways that are in your best interest and the interest of those you serve.

This is where the road splits. We need a new framework, one that's specifically designed for reputation management. It's a brand-new lock, and it requires a brand-new key.

ACKNOWLEDGMENTS

Every book is a journey. On this journey, I want to thank Allison Murray, who was there from the beginning and the bitter end as the keeper of the reputational excellence flame and taskmaster extraordinaire. If not for her nudges, deadlines, and cut-the-BS sincerity, this book would never have gotten out the door. Our colleagues Megan Skiles and Heather Siebel at Kith were always generous with perspective, encouragement, and assistance on research and special projects. Thank you both.

Every career is dotted with friends that make a difference. Thanks to the team at PSI and the dozens of hardworking, smart, and resilient strategic communicators that have been a part of many of the stories in this book. Some know the other stories that are better told over a beer and those that are better left untold; in particular, Allison, Amy, Blaine, Cliff, Danner, Eddie, Jack, Shannon, and Travis, thank you all for your friendship and partnership.

REFERENCES

Baer, Jay. 2016. *Hug Your Haters: How to Embrace Complaints and Keep Your Customers*. New York: Portfolio/Penguin.

Barnett, Michael L. and Sunyoung Lee. 2012. "The Role of Reputation in Reputation." *Saïd Business School Working Paper series*. https://www.sbs.ox.ac.uk/sites/default/files/SBS_working_papers/Reputation_complete.pdf.

Barnett, Michael L. and Sohvi Leih. 2016. "Sorry to (Not) Burst Your Bubble: The Influence of Reputation Rankings on Perceptions of Firms." *Sage Journals*. http://journals.sagepub.com/doi/abs/10.1177/0007650316643919.

Borden, Neil. 1957. "Note on Concept of the Marketing Mix." in Kelley, E.J. and W. Lazer (Eds.), *Managerial Marketing*. Homewood, IL: Durwin.

Branding Institute. 2017. *Ranking of the Rankings*. http://www.branding-institute.com/rating-the-rankings/ranking-of-the-rankings.

Burson-Marsteller Report: *CEO Reputation Study*. 2010. https://issuu.com/burson-marsteller-emea/docs/ceoreport.

Campbell, Mikey. 2017. "Apple's Corporate Reputation in Slow Decline, Market Research Suggests." *AppleInsider*. http://appleinsider.com/articles/17/02/28/apples-corporate-reputation-in-slow-decline-market-research-suggests.

Cole, Simon. 2012. "The Impact of Reputation on Market Value." *World Economics*. 13(3): 47–68.

Coleman, Les. 2004. "The Frequency and Cost of Corporate Crises." *Journal of Contingencies and Crisis Management*. 12(1): 2–13. http://onlinelibrary.wiley.com/doi/10.1111/j.0966-0879.2004.01201002.x/abstract.

Cuddy, Amy. 2015. *Presence: Bringing Your Boldest Self to Your Biggest Challenges*. New York: Little, Brown and Company.

Dale, Edgar. 1969. *Audio-Visual Methods in Teaching*. New York: Holt, Rinehart & Winston.

Davis, Scott. 2012. "Toyota: From Recalls to Relevance." *Forbes.com*. https://www.forbes.com/sites/scottdavis/2012/03/27/toyota-gets-drivers-of-reputation-and-cars/#410762251b09.

EOS. 2017. *The EOS Level 10 Meeting Agenda*. https://traction.eosworldwide.com/download-level10-agenda.

Frothingham, Steve. 2008. "Trek Announces an End to Deal with Greg LeMond." *velonews*. http://www.velonews.com/2008/04/news/trek-announces-an-end-to-deal-with-greg-lemond_74387.

Hyatt, David. 1950. *Introduction to Public Relations: A Practical Guide as Applied to Industrial and Labor Relations*. Ithaca, New York: Cornell University.

Indian River Admin. 2014. "Teubner—Corporate Value Driver #5: History and Reputation of the Firm." http://www.ir-advisors.com/ teubner-corporate-value-driver-5-history-reputation-firm/.

Johnson & Johnson. 2017. *Our Credo*. Accessed July 31, 2017. https:// www.jnj.com/about-jnj/jnj-credo.

Kaplan, Robert S. and Anette Mikes. 2012. "Managing Risks: A New Framework." *Harvard Business Review*. https://hbr.org/2012/06/ managing-risks-a-new-framework.

Lazauskas, Joe. 2016. *Fixing Native Ads: What Consumers Want from Publishers, Brands, Facebook, and the FTC*. The Tow-Knight Center for Entrepreneurial Journalism/Contently. https://the-content-strategist-13.docs.contently.com/v/ fixing-sponsored-content-what-consumers-want-from-brands-publishers-and-the-ftc.

Lesak-Greenberg, Kirsten. 2016. "#EpiGate: How Mylan is Handling Criticism Over Increased EpiPen Pricing." *The BuzzBin*. http://www.buzzbinpadillaco.com/ epigate-mylan-handling-criticism-increased-epipen-pricing/.

Maple Leaf Foods. 2017. "Maple Leaf Foods Pursuing Ambition to be the Most Sustainable Protein Company on Earth." *Company News Release*. June 6, 2017. http://www.mapleleaffoods.com/news/ maple-leaf-foods-pursuing-ambition-to-be-the-most-sustainable-protein-company-on-earth/.

McCarthy, E. Jerome. 1960. *Basic Marketing: A Managerial Approach*. Homewood, IL: R.D. Irwin.

Musil, Steven. 2017. "Apple and Samsung Take Hits to Their Reputations." *CNET*. February 28, 2017. https://www.cnet.com/news/ samsung-galaxy-note-7-apple-iphone-reputation-institute-2017/.

PwC. 2017. "Welcome to the Crisis Era. Are you Ready?" *CEO Pulse on Crisis*. http://www.pwc.com/gx/en/ceo-agenda/pulse/crisis.html.

Phyper, John and Paul MacLean. 2009. *Good to Green: Managing Business Risks and Opportunities in the Age of Environmental Awareness.* Ontario, Canada: Wiley.

Roth, Tom. 2013. *StrengthsFinder 2.0.* Washington, DC: Gallup Press.

Schreiber, Elliot S. 2017. *Essential Knowledge Reputation.* Center for Corporate Reputation Management Lebow. Accessed July 25, 2017: https://www2.lebow.drexel.edu/PDF/Docs/CCRM/EssentialKnowledge.pdf.

Shotfarm. 2016. "Is Product Content Helping or Hurting Your Brand?" *2015/16 Product Information Report.* http://www.shotfarm.com/product-information-report/.

Takeuchi, Hirotaka and John Quelch. 1983. "Quality is More than Making a Good Product." *Harvard Business Review,* July 1983.

Visser, Wayne. 2012. *Corporate Sustainability & Responsibility: An Introductory Text on CSR Theory & Practice – Past, Present & Future.* BookBaby.

Walmart. 2016. *More than One Million Walmart Associates to Receive Pay Increases in 2016.* http://news.walmart.com/news-archive/2016/01/20/more-than-one-million-walmart-associates-receive-pay-increase-in-2016.

Weinswig, Deborah. 2016. "Influencers Are the New Brands." *Forbes.* Oct. 5, 2016. https://www.forbes.com/sites/deborahweinswig/2016/10/05/influencers-are-the-new-brands/#7d26a2287919.

ABOUT THE
AUTHOR

BILL COLETTI is a crisis communications and reputation management expert with more than twenty-five years of global experience managing high-stakes crises, issues management, and media relations challenges for Fortune 500 companies and global political campaigns. He is the founder of Kith: a crisis communications and reputation management firm that is at its best when working with established corporations that feel disrupted in the age of disruption.

Bill previously co-led the Global Risk Management and Crisis Communications Practice for Hill+Knowlton Strategies and has provided senior counsel in crisis management, corporate communications, and reputation defense to clients, including AT&T, Cargill, the College Board, Target Corporation, American Airlines, The Home Depot, American Express, and Xerox, as well as universities and NGOs.